Measures for Adult Literacy Programs

Gregg B. Jackson

A joint publication of

The Association for Community Based Education

and

The ERIC Clearinghouse on Tests, Measurement, and Evaluation

Published by
The ERIC Clearinghouse on Tests, Measurement, and Evaluation
American Institutes for Research
3333 K Street, NW
Washington, DC 20007

Printed in the United States of America.

Preparation of this guide was funded with a grant from the John D. and
Catherine T. MacArthur Foundation to the Association for Community Based
Education. Publication support was provided by the Office of Educational
Research and Improvement (OERI), U.S. Department of Education, under
contract R-88-062003. The opinions expressed in this report do not necessarily
reflect the positions or policies of OERI, the MacArthur Foundation, the
Association for Community Based Education, or the American Institutes for
Research.

Library of Congress Catalog-in-Publication data

Jackson, Gregg B.

    Measures for adult literacy programs / Gregg B. Jackson.
    210 p.

    ISBN 0-89785-218-4
    1. Literacy programs -- United States -- Evaluation. 2. Adult education --
United States -- Evaluation. 3. Basic education -- United States -- Ability Testing.
I. ERIC Clearinghouse on Tests, Measurement, and Evaluation. II. Title.
LC151.J32 1990
374'.012--dc20
                                      90-34714
                                         CIP

ISBN 0-89785-218-4
First Printing August 1990

Preface

The importance of program outcome assessment is well recognized among practitioners in adult literacy programs. But few programs undertake rigorous or sustained evaluations. While lack of resources is one frequently mentioned reason, inability to locate appropriate instruments is another. Many programs have complained that they have not been able to find instruments that adequately reflect their purposes and missions.

There are however, many instruments that may be suitable for measuring adult literacy program outcomes. The Association of Community Based Education (ACBE) and the ERIC Clearinghouse on Tests, Measurement, and Evaluation are pleased to jointly sponsor *Measures of Adult Literacy* which describes some of these instruments. In this volume, Gregg Jackson provides candid evaluations of 63 measures that can be used to measure outcomes of adult literacy programs. Included are tests of basic reading, writing and mathematics skills, oral English proficiency, affective outcomes, and critical thinking. We feel the book is thorough, easy to read, and will be useful to a wide range of programs designed to improve adult literacy.

C.P. Zachariadis
Executive Director
Association for Community
   Based Education

Lawrence M. Rudner
Director
ERIC Clearinghouse on Tests,
   Measurement, and Evaluation

Contents

About this book

There are thousands of instruments for measuring human behavior. Only a few of them, especially the Tests of Adult Basic Education (TABE) and Adult Basic Learning Exam (ABLE), are widely known to persons concerned with adult literacy programs.

This book presents reviews of 63 instruments that are designed to measure student outcomes (impacts) considered important in these programs. The instruments include paper and pencil tests, structured interviews, and self-report forms.

These reviews have been written for administrators and teachers, as well as for evaluators and researchers. Technical terminology has been minimized. Characteristics of each instrument are reported in detail, with examples of the items to which students respond. Practical considerations are cited--such as the procedures for administering the instrument and the purchase costs. Notable strengths and weakness are highlighted.

The reviews can be used for several purposes. They can be used to find instruments appropriate for a given evaluation. They can be used to find background information on an instrument that is cited in a report or mentioned by a colleague. They can be used to defend against the imposition of ill-suited instruments by government authorities or funding agencies. They also can be used when developing one's own instruments--as a source of ideas on content, types of exercises, requirements for credible measurement, and pitfalls to be avoided.

The search for instruments was extensive. It focused on commercially available instruments and those developed by community based literacy programs. Only commercially available instruments are included in this guide. Reasons for that and details of the search are described in the Appendix.

Inclusion of an instrument in this guide does not mean that it is well suited for adult literacy programs. We tried to make the guide comprehensive within specified boundaries. The intent was to allow the reader to learn quickly about almost any commercially available instrument mentioned in connection with adult literacy. Then, based on the information provided in the review, the reader can make his or her own judgment of whether the instrument is a good candidate for a given purpose. Final decisions about the use of an instrument should be made after examining it carefully, reading the manual, and trying the instrument out with a few students.

Wise use of these instruments requires background knowledge that is not provided in this book or in the manuals that accompany most of the instruments. One who has not had professional training in measurement should at least read one of the texts on the subject. The most widely used are *Essentials of Psychological Testing* (L. Cronbach) and *Psychological Testing* (A. Anastasi). Another valuable source of guidelines is *Standards of Educational and Psychological Testing* (American Psychological Association).

The reviews are organized into four sections: Basic Skills--Reading, Writing, and Mathematics; Oral English Proficiency of ESL Students; Affective Outcomes; and Critical Thinking. Within each section, the reviews are arranged in alphabetical order by the full title. Acronyms follow many of the titles. Some instruments are commonly known by their acronym, not their full title. A detailed table of contents is provided at the beginning of each section. It also indicates the approximate reading skill level need to respond to the instrument. At the end of each section, there are references to additional instruments that were not reviewed because they are no longer available or because preliminary information suggested they are ill-suited for use in adult literacy programs.

Each review includes: the acronym for the instrument's title, authors and dates of publication, purpose, description of the exercises and scores, procedures for administration, alternate forms information, reliability data, validity data, procedures for scoring and interpretation, general comments, restrictions on availability, prices, and source of the instrument.

Author & Date

Often a range of dates is shown. The first date is when the instrument was introduced and the second date is when the latest version of the instrument or accompanying manual was published. Some publishers revise their instruments or update the manuals every five to ten years. As a consequence, the information in some of the reviews will become obsolete over time. A given version of a instrument is usually designated by the year of publication or by the "Form" number or letter. The "Alternate Forms" section of each review indicates which forms are described in the review.

Purpose

The reported purpose of the instrument was generally taken from the publisher's catalog or the manual that explains the instrument. Jargon was translated. In the few cases where the stated purpose was clearly more ambitious than can be achieved by the instrument, the claims were tempered.

Description

A description is given of the various types of items to which the student responds. Some instruments have many types, and space permitted describing just four or five. Examples of the items are presented. These examples are the ones provided to the student during the instructions, if there are such examples, or ones concocted by this author to represent the actual items. In no case are the actual instrument items revealed because about half of the instruments are "secured," as discussed below under "Availability." Some instruments result in several different scores. When that is the case, the names of all the scores are listed.

Administration

Some instruments must be administered to one student at a time; others can be administered to a group. Some are simple to administer and others are not. The reviewer tried to anticipate problems in administration by reading the instructions provided in the manual and examining the instrument, but he has not administered most of the instruments. If there is a time limit for responding to the instrument, it is reported. If there is no time limit, the amount of time needed by the slowest students is given--if it was cited in the manual or could reasonably be estimated by the reviewer. In both cases the times reported are just for responding to the instrument. Additional time is needed to give students the instructions and to distribute and collect the materials.

Alternate Forms

Some instruments, especially those that measure basic skills, are available at several levels of difficulty. Some are available in two or more equivalent forms for each level. One purpose of the equivalent forms is to minimize the effects of practice, when administering the instrument twice to the same students, such as would be done when assessing changes over time. When there were equivalent forms, the "Description" of the instrument is usually based on examining just one of the forms at each level. The other form will have similar items that measure the same outcomes.

Reliability

Reliability indicates the extent to which an instrument will give the same scores when administered twice to the same persons, before the traits being measured have changed. This is commonly judged by re-administering the instrument, and then correlating the scores of the first and second administration. This is called "test-retest reliability." Often reliability is judged by other analyses that are not strictly comparable. These analyses are used to provide estimates of the same underlying characteristic. Reliability is usually expressed as a correlation. Correlations below .5 indicate low reliability and values above .8 indicate high reliability.

Instruments with low reliability should always be avoided. Instruments with medium reliability are acceptable when the scores will be averaged for a group of students, as in program evaluations. This is because errors in scores tend to cancel out when several scores are averaged, thus making the average more reliable than the individual scores. Only instruments with high reliability should be used when making decisions about individual students, such as when assessing their individual needs or progress.

Validity

Validity indicates the extent to which the instrument actually measures the characteristics it is supposed to be measuring. There are many ways to assess validity and no single analysis adequately establishes an instrument's validity or lack thereof. The simplest manner of judging validity is to look at the instrument and decide whether it appears to be measuring the chosen characteristic. This is called "face validity" and is generally not given much credibility by professionals because there are many examples of instruments that appeared valid, but were later proven not to be. Relying of face validity is most justified when the instrument measures a skill directly--by means that are very similar to actual application of the skill in real life situations.

The reviews in this book primarily report concurrent, discriminate, and predictive validity. Concurrent validity is the extent to which the scores on the instrument correlate with those on some other well established measure of the characteristic. Discriminate validity is the extent to which the scores from the instrument vary among people in a way that would be expected from other knowledge. For instance, a measure of self-esteem would be suspect if the average score on it of persons who had recently tried to commit suicide was higher than the average score on it of reasonably happy persons. Predictive validity is the extent to which the scores on the instrument correlate with subsequent performance.

Validity is usually reported as a correlation. Correlations below .5 indicate low validity; correlations above .8 indicate high validity. Instruments with low validity should be avoided. Since validity generally increases when scores are averaged, instruments with medium validity can be used to make decisions about groups. They can also be used to make decisions about individuals when rough measures will suffice.

Scoring & Interpretation

Manual scoring (visually reviewing the responses, marking the errors, and calculating the scores) is simple and quick for some instruments and complex and time-consuming for others. When it is reported as "quick," it will not take more than one minute per copy of the instrument--once the scorer is experienced. Some publishers offer computerized scoring. It usually takes one or two weeks to get the results back, and the cost ranges from about $1.00- $8.00 per copy of the instrument. The advantages are the elimination of tedious work, increased accuracy in scoring, and the availability of sophisticated reports.

Well-developed instruments are usually accompanied by norms. Norms describe the distribution of scores achieved on the instrument by a large number of persons. That is useful because the raw scores on many instruments are difficult to interpret. What does a raw score of 15 out of 30 on a measure of oral proficiency mean? By itself, not much. But if we know that 90% of typical native English speaking first-graders score higher than 15 on this instrument, we know that it means a low level of proficiency.

Comments

This section reports other information about the instrument. Some of the instruments were specifically developed for adults and others were developed for elementary or high school students. The latter may appear juvenile and condescending to adults. Some instruments have a distinctly middle class orientation. Most of their items are about objects and activities not familiar to low-income adults.

Many of the instruments require some reading. The approximate level of reading required for responding to the instrument is reported. Sometimes the level reported is what is cited in the manual for the instrument. When the level was not cited, it was estimated by this reviewer after a brief examination of the instrument. The reviewer has considerable experience checking his own writing with the Flesch formula. There were several instances where he estimated the reading level and then later found it reported in the manual. The two values were usually within one grade level and never more than two grade levels apart. Extreme caution should be exerted in using reading formulas and reading levels. Reading is quite situational and adult readers are especially hard to categorize. Use the reported levels as an approximate guide which may not necessarily be valid for a particular literacy program.

The conclusions of prior published reviews of the instrument are reported if the instrument has not been revised since the review or if the conclusion is obviously applicable to the revision. Miscellaneous observations of this writer are also reported when they might be useful. An effort was made to identify both strengths and weaknesses.

Availability

Some instruments are "secured." That means that they are available for review and use only by professionals of certain qualifications, and they are to be stored and used with certain precautions. The required qualifications and the means of establishing one's qualifications vary among publishers and among different instruments of a given publisher. The restrictions reported are those stated by the publishers. Some are vague. When in doubt, submit a letter of inquiry to the publisher on the official stationery of your organization.

Price

The prices are as of 1988. They generally do not include postage and handling. Prices are given for the materials commonly necessary for administering the instrument: the student booklets, the response sheets, and the manual. Some instruments are accompanied by flip-cards, separate scoring keys, and other materials. Since some of these materials are optional and most require modest one-time expenses, their prices are not reported. Their availability is indicated in the publisher's catalogue. Prices usually change every year or two. Large orders may qualify for a discount of 10-20 percent.

A "specimen set" (sometimes called an "examination kit") is intended to permit a person to decide whether the instrument is suited for his or her purposes. It usually includes a copy of one form of the instrument and the answer sheet, and sometimes a copy of the manual. The price information indicates whether the manual is included. If not, it should be ordered when a specimen set is purchased. The information in the manual is essential for making intelligent judgments about an instrument.

Allow plenty of time when ordering materials. Order fulfillment normally takes 2-5 weeks unless you specify and pay for special shipment. Errors in filling orders are common (about ten percent of the orders for these reviews were initially filled incorrectly).

Source

The information reported was accurate as of 1988. Some instruments are distributed by two or more sources, but only the source used by this reviewer is listed.

Considerable effort was expended trying to make the reviews thorough, accurate, and helpful. But given the magnitude of the task, it is likely that some appropriate instruments are not included and that some important facts about reviewed instruments are missing. The reviewer welcomes suggestions for additions and changes. They should be sent to Gregg B. Jackson, c/o Association for Community Based Education, 1805 Florida Avenue, NW, Washington, DC 20009.

Basic Skills:
Reading, Writing
& Mathematics

Introduction

This section includes instruments that measure reading, mathematics, and writing. These different skills are covered together because several of the most widely used instruments measure all three. Also included, however, are several instruments that assess only one of the skills. Old instruments for measuring adult reading often relied solely on oral reading of progressively more difficult word lists. This measured decoding and word recognition skills, but not comprehension. Later instruments focused on silent reading of text--usually fiction or non-fiction material from academic disciplines such as history, geography, and life sciences. The passages were followed by multiple choice questions assessing comprehension of details--who, what, where, when, or how? The most modern instruments usually focus on silent reading, but the text and questions are different. The text is often material that many adults would find useful in their daily lives, such as rental agreements, utility bills, job advertisements, application forms, warranty cards, instructions for administering medication, newspaper articles, and magazine editorials. The questions are not only about details, but also about main ideas, the author's intentions, conclusions that can be inferred, and extrapolations that can be made to other situations.

Most of the instruments for measuring adult writing skills assess spelling, punctuation, capitalization, and grammar--using multiple choice questions. A few of the modern ones also include one or more writing assignments.

Instruments for measuring adults' basic math skills have changed little over the years. One section usually assesses computational skills--addition, subtraction, multiplication, division, decimals, fractions, and percentages. The second section usually has word problems that require summing numbers, calculating percentages, using unit prices, applying proportions, determining perimeters and areas of simple shapes, solving rate/time/quantity problems, and interpreting simple graphs and charts. Only rarely do these instruments assess number theory or require algebra.

In many adult literacy programs the range of participants' skills is such that it is desirable to have at least two levels of the instruments, one for persons with very elementary skills and one for persons with intermediate level skills. Many of the instruments reviewed in this section do have multiple levels.

The following table shows the instruments that are described in this section.

Instruments that Measure Basic Skills

Instrument	Page	What it measures	Reading requirements
Adult Basic Learning Exam (ABLE)	17	Reading, writing, and math	At least grade 2 reading
Adult Informal Reading Test (AIRT)	21	Reading	At least grade 1 reading
Basic Skills Assessment (BSA)	24	Reading, writing, and math	At least grade 7 reading
Botel Reading Inventory (BRI)	27	Reading and spelling	At least grade 1 reading
CASAS Adult Life Skills,	30	Reading	At least grade 1 reading
CAT Writing Skills Assessment System	33	Writing	No reading
Degrees of Reading Power (DRP)	36	Reading	At least grade 3 reading
EDS Diagnostic Skill Level Inventory for Writing Skills	39	Writing	At least grade 7 reading
General Education Performance Index (GEPI)	42	Reading, writing, math, and other	At least grade 8 reading
IOX Basic Skill Tests	45	Reading, writing, and math	At least grade 5 reading
Johnston Informal Reading Inventory (JIRI)	49	Reading	At least grade 2 reading

Instrument	Page	What it measures	Requirements
Language Assessment Scales-- Reading and Writing (LAS R/W)	52	Reading and writing	At least grade 2 reading
Life Skills	55	Reading and math	At least grade 8 reading
MAPS Self-Scoring Placement Tests (CGP)	58	Reading, writing, and math	At least grade 8 reading
McCarthy Individualized Diagnostic Reading Inventory	61	Reading	At least grade 2 reading
Michigan Test of English Language Proficiency (MTELP)	64	Reading and writing	At least grade 6 reading
Minimum Essentials Test (MET)	67	Reading, writing, math, and other	At least grade 6 reading
Objectives-Referenced Bank of Items & Tests (ORBIT)	69	Reading, writing, and math	At least kindergarten reading
Official GED Practice Tests	72	Writing, social studies, science, interpreting literature and the arts, math	At least grade 8 reading
Reading Evaluation Adult Diagnosis (READ)	75	Reading	At least grade 1 reading
Reading/Everyday Activities in Life (R/EAL)	77	Reading	At least grade 2 reading

Instruments that measure basic skills (continued)

Instrument	Page	What it measures	Requirements
Slosson Oral Reading Test (SORT)	80	Reading	At least grade 1 reading
Spanish Assessment of Basic Education (SABE)	82	Reading and math in Spanish	At least grade 1 reading
Spanish/English Reading Comprehension Test	84	Reading in Spanish and English	At least grade 1 reading
SRA Reading and Arithmetic Indexes	86	Reading and math	At least grade 1 reading
Test of Written Language (TOWL)	89	Writing	At least grade 5 reading
Tests of Adult Basic Education (TABE)	92	Reading, writing, and math	At least grade 2 reading
Test That's Not a Test (T-NAT)	95	Reading	At least grade 1 reading
Wide Range Achievement Test (WRAT-R)	97	Reading, spelling, and math	At least grade 1 reading
Woodcock-Johnson Psycho-Educational Battery	100	Reading, writing, math, and other	Some sections require no reading

Adult Basic Learning Examination (ABLE)

Author & Date

Bjorn Karlsen and Eric Gardner (1967-86)

Purpose

To measure basic education skills of adults.

Description

There are three levels of this instrument and they differ some in content as well as difficulty. Each has five or six sections. The vocabulary section has 32 items. A phrase is given and the student is asked to select which of three words completes it, providing a valid definition. An example is "A lizard is a kind of a) animal b) plant c)house." The reading section has 40-48 items. It assesses literal comprehension, inferences, and conclusions. At Level 1, some items present illustrations of signs with words and ask multiple choice questions about them; some present a series of related sentences, each of which has to be completed by selecting one of three words; and there are two short reading passages with multiple-choice questions. At Levels 2 and 3 there are ten reading passages or materials (including a warranty, a form, and a business letter). The spelling section has 30 items. At Level 1, the administrator dictates a word, uses it in a sentence, dictates it again, and then asks the student to write it down. In Levels 2 and 3 the student is to identify which of four printed words is misspelled. The language section (only in Levels 2 and 3) has 30 items. Some items ask the student to decide whether the underlined portion of a given sentence is correctly capitalized and punctuated, and if not, how it should be modified. The other items present a sentence with a blank within it, and ask the student to select which word or phrase "belongs in the blank." This assesses knowledge of English grammar. The section on number operations has 20-40 items, mostly involving addition, subtraction, multiplication, and division of whole numbers, fractions, decimals, and percentages. The section on problem solving has 20-40 word problems on totalling bills, calculating correct change, determining the savings from bulk prices, calculating net pay after withholding, ascertaining elapsed time, applying ratios, solving rate/unit/total problems, solving rate/time/quantity problems, using schedules, interpreting charts and graphs, and calculating perimeters/areas/volumes.

Administration

This instrument can be administered individually or to groups. The instructions are simple and clear. There is no time limit. Almost all students complete each section within 20 to 35 minutes. It is recommended that the sections be administered on different days or that students be given a 10 minute break between sections. The administrator provides the same instructions for comparable sections of Levels 2 and 3, so they can be simultaneously administered in one group. The instructions for Level 1, however, differ from those for Levels 2 and 3.

Alternate Forms

There are three Levels. Level 1 corresponds to grades 1-4; Level 2 corresponds with grades 5-8; and Level 3 corresponds with grades 9-12. There are two equivalent forms, E and F, of each level. In addition, there is a short screener that can be used to identify the appropriate level for each student.

Reliability

Test-retest reliability is not reported. KR-21 has been high (mostly .80 to .95).

Validity

Scores on this instrument have correlated moderately (.68 to .81) with comparable scores on the Stanford Achievement Test in a sample of 4th, 6th, 8th, and 10th grade youth.

Scoring & Interpretation

Manual scoring is moderately easy and takes about five minutes per instrument. For Level 1, the student answers the questions directly in the student booklet, rather than on a separate answer sheet. For Levels 2 and 3, one form of answer sheet has carbon paper on the back which transfers the marks to the back side of the answer sheet where the location of all correct marks is indicated. When the carbon paper is torn off, the answer sheet can be scored with no additional answer key or stencil. This permits self-scoring by the students. The printing on the back also permits scoring of sub-skills. For instance, reading comprehension can be scored for functional material and educational material, and for literal comprehension and inferential comprehension.

There are norm data based on 3,500 adults in 132 programs in 41 states. The norms are reported separately for ABE/GED students and for prisoners, as well as for a combination of both. More than half were of minority racial/ethnic groups. The first printing of the Level 2 Norms Booklet was accompanied by an extensive errata sheet.

Comments

This is a 1988 revision of an instrument that has been widely used to evaluate the outcomes of adult education. All the items are new and a third level has been added to measure skills equivalent to grade levels 9 to 12.

The instrument appears to be very responsive to several criticisms of prior instruments used in adult education programs. The content and tone are adult. The reading passages are mostly about common everyday matters and the questions tap not only literal comprehension, but also higher forms of comprehension. The mathematics word problems are the kinds many people encounter in daily life.

Ten of the 40 items in the reading section of Level 1 (Form E) appear to be flawed. Some of those ten cannot be answered correctly without background knowledge that a moderate portion of adult students probably will not possess. Two items require the students to know the purpose of steel-toed boots. Three items require knowing the appropriate actions to take when one detects a gas leak in a dwelling. Another requires knowing what will happen when the peelings from a pungent vegetable are thrown into a fire. The rest of the ten flawed items require predicting what an imaginary person did in a given situation, and there is no way to know for sure. To be scored as comprehending the item, the student must choose the option that would be the rational, safe, or common behavior. Since real people don't always act that way, is it reasonable to fault a student who fails to predict that they will?

For the mathematics word problems section, Level 1 requires no reading because all the problems are dictated. Level 2 requires about fourth grade reading and Level 3 requires about seventh grade reading. The Level 3 math section includes only very simple algebra and geometry problems. Some students who score high may find themselves required to take remedial math when enrolling in technical schools and colleges. This reviewer has substantial experience in administering level 2 and 3 of the reading comprehension section, and levels 1, 2, and 3 of the problem solving section, to adult literacy students. He is generally pleased with how the instrument has worked. The students do not appear offended by the instrument, and they seem to apply themselves.

The manual indicates that students "be encouraged to try to answer every question, even when they are not positive of the correct answer. They should also be alerted to the fact that there may be questions they cannot answer and that this should not worry them." The specific instructions that are read to the students, however, do not incorporate these suggestions. Since the manual also indicates the instructions should be supplemented "with explanations whenever necessary," these suggestions should be added to them.

Availability
This instrument will be sold to staff of most educational programs if the request is on official stationary or an official purchase order.

Price
Fifty screener instruments cost $21.00 to $48.00. Twenty-five student booklets for Level 1, 2, or 3 cost $30.00 (Level 1 booklets are not reusable.) Fifty answer sheets for Levels 2 and 3 cost $21.00 to $48.00. The manual (called "Norms Booklet") costs $13.00 (and there is a separate one for each level of the instrument). A specimen set, with the instruments for each of the three levels and instructions for administering them, but not with a copy of the Norms Booklet, costs $21.00.

Source

The Psychological Corporation
555 Academic Court
San Antonio, TX 78204-0952
(512) 299-1061

Adult Informal Reading Test (AIRT)

Author & Date
Robert E. Leibert (1969-1980)

Purpose
To estimate instructional needs and assess changes in reading.

Description
There are two sections. One has six word lists of 20-30 words each, and the student is to read the words aloud. The easiest list has words like "boy" and "go." The most difficult list has words like "northeast" and "contender." The lists are in large print. The second section has six short reading passages ranging in difficulty from about the grade 1 level to about the grade 9 level. Performance on the word lists is used to select the first passage to be read. The student is asked to read each passage aloud and remember it, so he or she can answer questions about it afterwards. The oral reading is judged in respect to accuracy of word recognition and rate of reading. The passage is then taken back by the administrator and the student is asked five questions about details in the passage--mostly who, what, and how?.

Administration
The instrument must be administered individually. The instructions are moderately complex and not entirely clear. Though the rate of reading is used to judge the student's performance, the student is not forewarned on that fact. On the contrary, the administrator is admonished that, "The adult should not be caused to believe that this is a speed test." The administrator is supposed to record the nature of all mistakes, and keep track of how much time the student takes to read the passages, without the student being aware of the timekeeping! There is no time limit, but ten to twenty minutes will probably be required.

Alternate Forms
There is only one form of the word lists, but there are two approximately equivalent forms of the reading passages. They are labeled as forms A and B.

Reliability

No reliability data are reported in the manual.

Validity

The manual provides only limited data on the validity of this instrument. The reading difficulty of the passages was determined with the Spache or Dale-Chall readability formulas. In addition, it was empirically determined that each passage results in more word recognition errors than the passage at the next lower level, when read aloud by adults in ABE classes. There are serious questions about the validity of this instrument. Most real-life reading is done silently, not aloud. It is quite conceivable that some adults will perform considerably less well when reading aloud than they can when reading silently. It is the test developer's responsibility to provide evidence that performance on a proxy task is a good indicator of performance on the real-life task. No such evidence is provided in the manual.

Removing the reading passage, before questioning the student about it, makes the questions a measure of both comprehension and memory. In addition, many of the comprehension questions for three of the six passages in Form A and two of the six passages in Form B can be answered correctly from common prior knowledge without reading the passages.

Scoring & Interpretation

Scoring is difficult and time consuming. The instructions for scoring are incomplete. All errors during the oral reading of the passages are to be recorded by the administrator. According to a footnote to an example of such recording, only certain kinds of the errors are to be counted when determining the accuracy of the reading. No norms are reported. Instead a system for judging the student's "Reading Practice Level" and "Peak Functional Level" is provided. The former is the level "where the reading performance deviates from almost perfect performance." The latter is "the highest level which can be read with adequate comprehension (60 percent)."

Comments

This instrument was developed for adults. It is designed to measure reading at about grade levels 1-10.

Availability

The instrument is available to anyone.

Price

One copy of the instruments and manual are free. The copyright has been waived; the instruments may be duplicated as long as proper credit is given on each copy.

Source

Robert E. Leibert
School of Education
University of Missouri-Kansas City
5100 Rockhill Road
Kansas City, MO 64110-2499
(816) 276-2480

Basic Skills Assessment
(BSA)

Author & Date

Samuel A. Livingston and Michael J. Zieky (1977-81)

Purpose

To measure specific competencies in reading, writing, and mathematics, as they apply to everyday situations.

Description

There are sections on reading, writing, and mathematics. The reading section measures literal comprehension, inference, evaluation, and total competency. There are 65 multiple choice items. Short reading passages and life-skills materials are followed by one to three questions. The materials include a medicine label, map, bus schedule, job ad, job application, loan agreement, warranty, tax form, and newsletter editorial.

The writing section measures spelling, capitalization, punctuation, usage, logic-evaluation, and total competency. There are 75 multiple choice items and an optional set of writing assignments. In the multiple choice items, students are asked to indicate which of four underlined words in a short paragraph is misspelled; which of four underlined letters and punctuation marks in a given sentence has an error in punctuation or capitalization; what necessary information is missing from an addressed envelope; which of four alternatives best fits in the blank of a given sentence; which of four alternative sets of words could correctly join two given sentences into one; which of four alternative sentences is the best for a stated purpose; and which of four alternatives would best edit a specified part of a given paragraph. The optional writing assignments include filling in an application form, drafting a letter in response to a job announcement, preparing an announcement, and writing a brief article for a school newspaper.

The math section provides scores for computation, application, and total competency. There are 70 multiple choice items. The computations focus on basic operations with whole numbers, decimals, fractions, and percentages. The word problems involve averages, proportions, time/rate/quantities, needed postage, and the interpretation of charts and graphs.

Administration

The instrument may be administered individually or to groups. The instructions are simple and clear, but no examples are given to the students. The administration may be timed or not. A forty-five minute time limit is suggested for each of the three sections

Alternate Forms

There are three forms, A, B, and C.

Reliability

Test-retest reliability is not reported in the manual. KR-20 has been moderate to high (.73 to .91) for the subscores (such as literal comprehension and inference) and high (.92 to .95) for the total reading, writing, and math scores.

Validity

The scores on this instrument have correlated moderately with teachers' end of the year assessments as to whether the students need remedial work in the three skill areas. In all cases, the scores increased between grades 8 and 9, and between grades 9 and 12. The reading and writing scores have correlated moderately highly (.75 to .81) suggesting that these two sections measure some common skills.

Scoring & Interpretation

Manual scoring is moderately complex because there is a separate scoring template for each of the eight subscores and then the subscores have to added to get the total scores for reading, writing, and math. Scoring will take several minutes for each student because of this and the large number of items. Computerized scoring is available from the publisher. There are norm data based on 7,731 high school students in 203 schools across the country.

Comments

This instrument was designed for high school students and adults. The reading and writing sections provide a broad sample of materials that confront most adults. Though the math section also provides a wide range of word problems found in daily life, those that are most commonly encountered are curiously missing. There is no question about the correct change for a given transaction, no question about the total cost of a purchase with installment plan interest charges, and no problem about the monthly earnings that result from a specified hourly rate. The reading required for the math section is at about the fifth grade level; the reading required for the reading and writing sections is at about the seventh grade level.

Two 1985 reviews (in The Ninth Mental Measurements Yearbook, #122) generally praised this instrument for purposes of assessing the three R's in application to life coping tasks.

Availability

The instrument will be sold to teachers "in institutions or agencies with signed approval on the CTB order form of his or her administrator."

Price

Thirty-five reusable student booklets, including the reading, writing, and arithmetic instruments, cost $64.75. One hundred answer sheets cost $18.00. A User Guide costs $5.75 and a separate Technical Manual also costs $5.75. A specimen set, including Directions for Administration, but not the User Guide or Technical Manual, costs $10.00.

Source

Publishers Test Service
CTB/McGraw-Hill
2500 Garden Road
Monterey, CA 93940
(800) 538-9547, or (408) 649-8400 from outside the continental United States

Botel Reading Inventory
(BRI)

Author & Date

Morton Botel (1961-78)

Purpose

To measure several component skills of reading.

Description

There are four sections, with a separate score for each. The first section measures decoding skills. It has 120 items. The student is asked to indicate which of five written letters in a set is the one named orally by the administrator, to indicate which of five written words in a set begins with the same sound as two words presented orally by the administrator, to indicate which of five written words in a set rhymes with two words presented orally by the administrator, and to read aloud words on nine progressively more difficult lists. The second section measures spelling. It has five lists, each with twenty words. The student is asked to write down words orally presented by the administrator. The easiest words are like "run" and "dog;" the hardest are like "connect" and "strawberry." The third section measures word recognition. It has eight lists, each with twenty words. The student is asked to read aloud words on progressively more difficult lists. The easiest words are like "cat" and "rug;" the most difficult are like "creative" and "pressure." The forth section measures understanding of word meaning through recognition of word opposites. There are ten sets of items, each with ten items. The student is to indicate which of three written words "means the opposite or nearly the opposite" of a given written word.

Administration

Administration of this instrument is moderately complex. The last part of the decoding section and all of the word recognition section must be administered individually. The first part of the decoding section, and all of the spelling and word opposites sections can be administered to groups. Progressively more difficult sets of items are given until the student fails to complete correctly 80% in two successive sets, 80% on one set, or 70% on two successive sets, depending on the section. No rationale is given for these different termination criteria. There is no time limit and the manual does not indicate how much time most students need. Explicit instructions for the students are not given in the manual; the tasks are simple and apparently the administrator is to improvise instructions.

Alternate Forms

There is only one form of the decoding and spelling sections. There are two approximately equivalent forms of the word recognition and word opposites sections; they are designated Test A and Test B.

Reliability

Test-retest reliability, using the two alternate forms, has generally been high (mostly .80 to .98). Internal consistency, as conventionally defined, is not reported. The scores on the word recognition section and the word opposites section have correlated highly (.86 to .95) for children in grades 1-3.

Validity

Scores on this instrument have correlated moderately and highly (mostly .57 to .95) with school principals' and teachers' judgments of student performance in basal reading texts. (There is an error in the manner in which these correlations were calculated; if corrected, the correlations would be higher.)   Scores on this instrument have correlated highly (.78 to .94) with informal reading inventories for which grade levels were established by the Spache, Dale-Chall, and Botel readability measures. Correlations with unspecified standardized reading tests have been moderate to high (mostly .55 to .93)

Scoring & Interpretation

Manual scoring is fairly simple and requires only two or three minutes per student. Limited norm data are provided. They are based on 659 elementary pupils in one Pennsylvania school during 1968.

Comments

This instrument was designed for elementary school children. The vocabulary was selected to be representative of elementary school primers. Some adults may find it condescending or boring.

The first and second section of this instrument are used for diagnosis of pre-reading skills. Only the sections on word recognition and word opposites are used to determine reading skill. The word recognition section, however, is quite easy. In one study, half of all third graders got a perfect score.

Availability

The instrument will be sold to anyone.

Price

Thirty-five response sheets for the decoding section cost $7.71. Thirty-five response sheets for the word recognition section or word opposites sections cost $9.00. The manual, with copies of all the instruments, costs $10.25.

Source

Modern Curriculum Press
13900 Prospect Road
Cleveland OH 44136
(800) 321-3106

CASAS Adult Life Skills--Reading (Forms 31-36) (CASAS Survey Achievement Tests)

Author & Date

California Adult Student Assessment System (1984-89)

Purpose

To assess a student's ability to apply basic reading skills in everyday life situations.

Description

There are 24 to 38 items, depending on which level of the instrument is used. All are multiple choice. The items require reading and answering questions about clocks, signs, labels, charts, maps, bank checks, forms, job advertisements, product advertisements, first aid instructions, how-to instructions, rental agreements, and business letters. One example at Level A shows a clock and asks, "What is this? a) Calendar b) Clock c) Map d) Money." An item at Level C presents a brief news story of yesterday's weather and asks how much rain fell. Most of the items assess literal comprehension. Few of the items require inferences or evaluation. There is just one score, the total number correct.

Administration

The instrument can be administered individually or to groups. The instructions are simple and clear. There is no time limit. Most students finish within 60 minutes.

Alternate Forms

There are several levels. Levels AA, AAA, and AAAA are for developmentally disabled students. Levels A, B, and C are suitable for most beginning, intermediate, and moderately advanced adult basic education students. Level C is substantially easier than the GED test. There are two approximately equivalent forms for each level. At Level A they are Forms 31 and 32; at Level B they are Forms 33 and 34; and at Level C they are forms 35 and 36.

All CASAS instruments are prepared from the CASAS item bank that now has 4,000 items. The item bank allows quick and relatively inexpensive construction of customized instruments for given purposes and given difficulty levels.

Reliability

The manual and other materials provided by the publisher do not report test-retest reliability. Internal reliability, measured by KR-20 has been high (.88 to .89).

Validity

Data showing correlations between scores on this instrument and other measures of reading were not provided by the publisher, despite three requests for validity data.

Scoring & Interpretation

Manual scoring is simple and quick. Raw data are converted to standard scores. The publisher does not report norms in percentiles or grade equivalents. There are, however, data for average entry, exit, and gains, from programs throughout California.

Comments

This instrument is used widely in California state-funded adult basic education programs and English as a Second Language programs. It is also used elsewhere.

The instrument is adult in content and tone. Virtually all of the reading materials and tasks are things that most adults would find useful in the course of everyday living.

The content, however, is exclusively life skill oriented. There are no items that assess the kinds of reading passages commonly found in popular magazines, newspapers, and books. Though CASAS is described as a competency-based assessment system, these instruments are not suited to assessing specific competencies. That is because the specified competencies are broad in scope and seldom measured by more than three items. For instance, in Form 31 of Level A, the competency of "interpret food packaging labels" is assessed by just one item, the competency of "identify the months of the year and the days of the week" is assessed by only two items, and the competency of "ask for, give, follow, or clarify directions" is assessed by only two items.

The items not only require reading life-skill material (signs, labels, warranties, etc.), but also reading the questions about them and the response choices. For several of the items at Level A, the reading that is required to comprehend the question and the response choices is at a higher level than required for the life-skill material. For instance, the item might show a picture of a conventional traffic stop sign and ask: "What does this sign mean? a) Caution b) Halt before proceeding c) Keep out d) Don't smoke." Some people who know what a stop sign means won't be able to read the question and the response choices. As a consequence, level A of the instrument will under-estimate very elementary survival reading.

31

Availability

This instrument is available to educational organizations, but a member of their staff must go through training provided by CASAS before using it.

Price

Twenty-five student booklets of one form cost $30.00. An extensive manual is provided during the required training. Write or call for information on the cost of the training.

Source

CASAS
2725 Congress Street, #1-M
San Diego, CA 92110
(619) 298-4681

CAT Writing Skills Assessment System

Author & Date
CTB/McGraw-Hill (1986-1987)

Purpose
To assess writing skills.

Description
This system directly assesses writing skills--by analyzing student writing in response to standardized topics. There are eight levels of topics, suitable for students in grades 2 through 12. At the lower levels, two types of writing can be assessed--descriptive and narrative. At the higher levels, three types of writing can be assessed--expository, narrative, and persuasive. There is a different topic for each type and level (a total of 21 prompts). The topics are like: 1) "Think about the hardest thing you have done in life. Describe what it was like and why it was hard." 2) "Imagine that you could have any life you wanted. Write a story about what happened in that life." and 3) "Think about examples of a leader. Explain what qualities make a good leader."

Administration
This instrument can be administered individually or to groups. The instructions are simple and clear. There is a 35 minute time limit, but most students stop writing before then.

Alternate Forms
There is only one topic for each level and type of writing.

Reliability
Test-retest reliability is not reported. Inter-scorer reliability, which only indicates the reliability of the scoring, has been mostly moderate (between .5 and .7). Test-retest reliability is likely to be somewhat less than those figures.

Validity
Limited validity data are reported. The holistic scores have low to moderate correlations with the language mechanics and language expression scores of the California Achievement Test (mostly .4 to .7). This is not very convincing evidence of validity. The latter scores are from multiple choice items, and the main rationale for assessing writing samples is that multiple choice items are mediocre indicators of actual

33

writing skill. Correlations between the holistic scores for different topics at a given level of the instrument have been moderate (between .50 and .71). Since test-retest reliability is not likely to be much more than those values, the different types of topics apparently elicit similar writing skills.

Scoring & Interpretation

Scoring is complex and will require considerable training and monitoring if it is to be done reliably. The publisher, however, offers scoring by its own team of trained readers who have scored thousands of these writing samples. The scoring is based on the following five criteria: 1) content (focus, logic, and detail), 2) organization (order and coherence), 3) sentence construction, 4) vocabulary and grammar, and 5) spelling and capitalization. The scoring can be done holistically, with reference to all the criteria at once. It also can be done analytically, in reference to any one or more of the criteria, each judged individually.

There is a separate manual explaining the scoring for each topic. It not only describes the criteria and provides examples of scored compositions, but it also outlines the logistics that will be needed to train local scorers. After reading the manual, the publisher's scoring service will seem well worth the cost. When this service is used, a computer readable form must be filled in for each student. Low level students may need a staff person to do it for them.

Comments

This direct assessment of writing was developed for elementary and secondary school students. Many of the topics, however, are relevant to adults and provide an opportunity for self-reflection and critical thinking.

This reviewer has substantial experience administering the Level 15 and 16 expository topics (grades 4 - 7) in adult literacy programs. The problems that were noticed are the following: the students seldom planned their writing, seldom wrote for more than the allotted time, and seldom put down more than 150 words (even after seven months of classes). This may reflect the students' writing styles and the training provided to them, rather than shortcomings in the instrument, but the matter deserves further investigation.

Availability

This instrument will be sold to teachers "in institutions or agencies with signed approval on the CTB order form of his or her administrator." The catalogue says that some instruments require secure handling, but it doesn't indicate which ones.

Price

Thirty-five non-reusable booklets for any one topic, plus the Administration and Scoring Manual, cost $18.00. The packages of booklets are not sold without the manual. The Writing Assessment Guide, with very limited reliability and validity data, costs $12.00; this guide also suggests a range of activities for improving writing skills.

Fifty computer readable forms, the ones that must be filled in when using the publisher's scoring service, cost $9.50. The publisher's scoring service costs $3.50 per student for holistic scoring, and a dollar more for each analytical score.

Source:

Publishers Test Service
CTB/McGraw-Hill
2500 Garden Road
Monterey, CA 93940
(800) 538-9547, or (408) 649-8400 from outside the continental United States

Degrees of Reading Power
(DRP)

Author & Date
(1979-86)

Purpose
To measure ability to understand nonfiction text at various levels of difficulty.

Description
This is a series of instruments using the same format, but with increasingly difficult reading material. Each instrument is comprised of eight or eleven passages on non-fiction subjects. Each is about 325 words long. Seven sentences in each passage have a blank indicating a missing word, and the student is to select the most appropriate choice from five given alternatives. All the alternatives are common words, semantically plausible, and syntactically correct, but only one is consistent with the meaning of the passage. The passages are arranged in the booklets in order of increasing difficulty. The following is part of one example passage: "It was sunny and hot for days. Then the _____1_____ changed. It turned cloudy and cool. a) price b) road c) job d) weather e) job"

Administration
The instrument can be administered individually or to groups. The instructions to the students are simple and clear. The instrument is not timed; most students complete it within 50 minutes.

Alternate Forms
There are five levels of the instrument and two equivalent forms of each. There is also a form PX-1 that may be given to students to practice doing this type of exercise and to screen for the appropriate level of the instrument.

Reliability
Alternate forms of the instrument were given to fourth and sixth graders twice, with one to two weeks in between. The correlations were high (.86 to .91) indicating that the forms were indeed closely equivalent and that test-retest reliability would be high. KR-20 coefficients were also high (.94 to .97).

Validity

The correlation between the DRP and a similar instrument that required generating a response (rather than selecting from five given alternatives) was high (.90). Correlations with the reading scores of the 1977 California Achievement Test were mostly high (.77 to .85).

Scoring & Interpretation

The answer sheets can be manually scored easily. There is just one raw score, the total number correct. That score is converted to DRP units by referring to the conversion table for the form used. Computerized scoring is also available from the publisher. There is norm data for 3rd through 12th graders based on more than 34,000 students in the state of New York.

Comments

This series of instruments was designed to be appropriate for youth and adults reading at about grades 3 to 14. The content and format of the easiest form of the instrument would not be considered condescending by most adults, but the reading passages are not likely to be of high interest to low-income adults. For instance, in form PX-1 there are reading passages on seeing-eye dogs, what police doctors can learn from skeletons, and the differences between true hibernation and pseudo-hibernation.

This instrument primarily assesses literal and inferential comprehension. It does not assess skills such as evaluation, interpretation, and application of what is read.

There is a trick aspect to several of the items. The correct response is most obvious only after reading one or two sentences beyond the sentence in which the word is missing. The instructions given to the students don't preclude reading all of the passage before answering the item, but they do not suggest that approach. Most students will probably catch on to the trick and adjust to it, especially since the instructions do state that answers can be changed and there is no time limit. But some students at the lowest reading levels may not detect the trick and score substantially lower than they could have when aware of it.

Availability

Individuals operating adult education programs may purchase the DRP instruments only if they have the training and experience to use them with professional care. DRP instruments and scoring keys must be kept in locked files or storage cabinets accessible only to authorized personnel.

Price

Thirty-five reusable booklets cost $45.25. Forty answer sheets cost $7.50. The manual with administration instructions costs $13.95. A specimen set costs $15.00.

Source

TASA
DRP Services
Fields Lane, P.O. Box 382
Brewster, NY 10509
(914) 277-4900

EDS Diagnostic Skill Level Inventory For Writing Skills

Author & Date
R. Lee Henney (1975-1978)

Purpose
To assess six categories of writing skills.

Description
The instrument has six sections, each of which is scored separately. There are a total of 65 items. The section on grammatical usage asks the student to indicate which of four underlined words in a sentence is "incorrectly used." The section on mechanics asks the student to mark which of four underlined parts of a sentence contains incorrect punctuation or capitalization. The section on spelling asks the student to indicate which of four words is misspelled. The section on sentence structure asks the student to indicate which of four endings to a sentence "completes the sentence most effectively and employs correct sentence structure." The section on diction and style asks the student to identify which of four sentences "is faulty because of inaccurate or ineffective word choice," (most of the faulty words are incorrect homophones--words that sound the same but are spelled differently and have different meanings). The section on logic and organization asks the student to indicate which of four endings "completes the sentence most effectively, clearly, and employs correct English."

Administration
The instrument can be administered individually or to groups. The instructions are simple. There is a one hour time limit for all six sections together. Apparently most students can finish within that limit. The manual says that when sessions without time limits were compared with this time limit, there was no effect on the students' scores.

Alternate Forms

There are two forms, parallel in content. One is called Pre-Instructional and the other is called Post-Instructional.

Reliability

Test-retest reliability is not reported in the manual. Split-half and KR-20 reliability have been high (.86 to .96) for 500 adult education students.

Validity

This instrument has been validated against the GED exam. The results reported in the manual are difficult to interpret. The manual says 94 percent of those who passed the GED writing section scored "average or above average in all categories" of this instrument. That is not a sufficient means of judging validity. At the very least the manual should also report the percent of those who didn't pass the GED writing test who scored below average on this instrument.

Scoring & Interpretation

Manual scoring is simple and quick. There is a table that shows which scores on each section of the instrument are "good," "average," "need study," and "study intensely." The cutoff between "average" and "need study" apparently is roughly equivalent to the minimum pass score on the writing section of the GED, but there is some confusion in the manual about that. No adequate norm data are reported in the manual.

Comments

Some of the sentences used in the exercises have adolescent content, but most are appropriate for adults. The exercises require reading at about the seventh grade level.

There are two unusual features of this instrument that suggest a lack of sophistication in developing measurement tools. First, the front cover of the student booklet is labeled "Pre-Instructional Test" or "Post-Instructional Test," depending on which of the two forms it is. That label might influence student effort and performance. The common practice is to label forms as "1, 2, or 3," or as "A, B, & C" to make that notation meaningless to the students. Second, the table that shows which scores are good, average, etc, is printed on the front cover of the student booklet. A student, who finds he or she doesn't know the answer to several questions in a section, could be rattled by the information.

Availability

This instrument is available to everyone.

Price

Twenty copies of reusable student booklets cost $16.00. One hundred answer sheets cost $10.00. A specimen set, including a copy of the manual, costs $6.25.

Source

Educational Diagnostic Services
P.O. Box 347
Valparaiso, IN 46383
(219) 462-2239

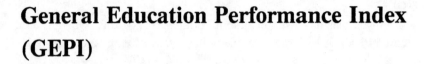

General Education Performance Index (GEPI)

Author & Date
Don F. Seaman and Anna C. Seaman (1981)

Purpose
To predict a student's success on the GED examination.

Description
There are five sections--writing, reading, mathematics, social studies, and science--each with a separate score. That is also the case with the GED examination.

The writing section has a total of 40 items. It includes exercises on spelling (identify which of four given words is misspelled); capitalization (indicate which of four underlined letters in a given sentence is improperly capitalized or not capitalized); punctuation (indicate which of four underlined portions of a given sentence is incorrectly punctuated); English usage (indicate which of four underlined words or phrases in a given sentence contains an error of grammar, word choice, structure or style); sentence structure (indicate which of four given strings of words best completes a sentence); and paragraph analysis (answer questions about needed edits to given paragraphs--questions like "Sentence 5 should be a) moved to beginning of paragraph b) put after sentence 6 c) omitted)."

The reading section has 27 questions about eight short passages from a story, a Shakespearean play, literary criticism, an editorial, and a list of reference publications. The student is asked multiple-choice questions about details in the passages, the main ideas, and inferences. Several of the passages are written at about the tenth grade level and deal with esoteric matters.

The mathematics section has 23 computation and word problems. The computation problems include multiplying several fractions, converting a whole number and fraction to an improper fraction, adding positive and negative numbers, finding the square root, calculating the value of an algebraic expression when the values of A and B are given, and subtracting two algebraic expressions. The word problems involve reading charts and graphs, using unit prices, converting scales, calculating the percent profit on a sale, and calculating the dollar amount of earned interest.

Administration

The instrument can be administered individually or to groups. The instructions are simple and clear. There is no time limit. Most students finish all five sections within four hours.

Alternate Forms

There are two approximately equivalent forms, AA and BB.

Reliability

Test-retest reliability has been moderate to high (.67 to .83) when using the two different forms (AA first and then BB, or vice versa).

Validity

The scores on this instrument correlated moderately (.61 to .73) with scores on the GED test that was in use until the late 1980s.

Scoring & Interpretation

Manual scoring is simple, but takes a few minutes because of the large number of items. Norm data are based on 615 adult education students from fifteen states. About half were minority.

Comments

This instrument was developed to predict whether a student is likely to pass the GED test, thus saving students from unnecessary registration fees and the distress of failing that exam. The content and tone is adult. The orientation is middle class and academic, but that is appropriate since the same is true of the GED test. Most of the items on this instrument require high school level skills. Students with less than about an eighth grade level of reading will have a tough time.

This instrument was developed and validated before the recent and fairly substantial revisions in the GED tests. Because of that, it probably is not as good a predictor of GED test performance as it used to be.

Availability

The instrument will be sold to anyone.

Price

Ten reusable student booklets cost $33.75. Fifty answer sheets cost $13.48. A specimen set, including a copy of the manual, costs $9.99.

Source

Steck-Vaughn
P.O. Box 2028
Austin, TX 78768
(800) 531-5015, or (800) 252-9317 in Texas

IOX Basic Skill Tests

Author & Date
The Instructional Objectives Exchange (1978-79)

Purpose
To measure mastery of specific skills in the areas of reading, writing, and mathematics.

Description
There are two levels of this instrument, elementary and secondary. Each includes sections on reading, writing, and mathematics, but the specific skills measured differ some between the two levels. All items are the multiple choice type, except for one writing sample required in the writing section.

The reading section at the elementary level presents sentences and paragraphs about everyday events and asks 35 questions about them. Seven competencies are assessed. The part on comprehending words uses a word in a sentence, and then asks which of three given statements provides the "best meaning" for the word. The part on comprehending syntax presents a sentence and then asks a question about it. The part on identifying details presents paragraphs and asks questions about what, where, and how. The part on identifying sequences presents paragraphs and asks what happens just before or right after some specified event. The part on determining main ideas presents paragraphs and asks what is the main idea. The part on using a dictionary presents a word in a sentence, and then asks which of the four definitions best fits the usage in the sentence. The part on using reference materials presents a schedule, map, etc. and asks questions that can be answered with them.

The reading section at the secondary level presents many short reading materials and asks 30 questions about them. Five competencies are assessed. The part on following written instructions presents paragraphs on first aid and safety, and asks what is the proper action in a given predicament. The part on completing forms and applications presents such materials and asks which of the given alternatives is an appropriate response for a given place on the form. The part on using reference sources presents a table of contents, a telephone directory, and a map, and asks questions that are to be answered with them. The part on determining the main ideas presents a descriptive paragraph and asks for the best statement of the main idea. The part on using everyday documents presents a credit card agreement, warranty, voting instructions, and first aid instructions, and asks what you need to do for a specified purpose.

The writing section at the elementary level has a total of 36 items that assess eight competencies. The part on identifying complete sentences presents three statements and asks which is a complete sentence. The part on spelling presents three sentences, each with one underlined word, and asks which is misspelled. The parts on capitalization, punctuation, verbs, adverbs and adjectives, and pronouns are similar. Each presents a set of three sentences and asks which one contains a mistake in the characteristic being assessed. The part on expressing ideas in writing asks the student to write a paragraph of at least four sentences on a specified topic. The student is forewarned to use complete sentences, and correct spelling, punctuation, and capitalization.

The writing section at the secondary level has a total of 20 items that assess four competencies. The part on using words correctly presents a sentence and asks which of four others would be grammatically correct following the first sentence. The part on checking mechanics presents a brief passage, with each line numbered, and asks which of three stated corrections, if any, needs to be made. The section on selecting correct sentences presents a sentence or two and asks which of four others would be "correctly-written" following the first one(s). The part on expressing ideas in writing presents four controversial topics, each with a brief explanation of two opposing views. The student is asked to write a paragraph explaining "why you are in favor or opposed to" one of the views. The student is warned to use a topic sentence stating his or her side of the argument, have all sentences support the topic sentence, use correct grammar, spelling, and punctuation, and "pay special attention to clear handwriting."

The math section at the elementary level assesses six competencies with a total of 30 questions. The first three parts involve basic computations with whole numbers, fractions, and decimals. The two parts on word problems require totalling a bill, calculating the proper change, computing proportions, solving rate/time/quantity problems, and reading rulers and thermometers. The part on reading tables and graphs involves simple interpretation of these displays.

The math section at the secondary level assesses four competencies with a total of 25 questions. The part on basic calculations involves addition, subtraction, multiplication and division of whole numbers, decimals and fractions. The three parts on word problems requiring totalling a bill, calculating the change due from a purchase, budgeting, calculating the miles per gallon achieved by a car, calculating the net deposit to a checking account, totalling a mail order form, calculating the discounted prices and commissions based on a specified percentage, calculating a perimeter, solving a rate/time/quantity problem, and calculating how much extra a purchase will cost if made on an installment basis rather than paid in full at the time of purchase.

Administration

The instrument can be administered individually or to groups. The instructions are simple and clear. There are no time limits. Most students will complete any one of the sections within 50 minutes.

Alternate Forms

There are two forms, A and B, at both the elementary and secondary level. They are said to be approximately equivalent.

Reliability

Test-retest reliability for the individual competency scores at the secondary level has generally been moderate (mostly .60 to .70). There were, however, two important departures from good practice when collecting this data; the correct values are probably .50 to .65. The KR-20 has also generally been moderate (mostly .60 to .80). Reliability for the total reading, writing, and math scores is not reported in the manual but would be higher than the values reported immediately above.

Validity

The manuals do not report correlations between the scores on this instrument and other measures of the skills. They acknowledge the need for further validation studies, but the results were not provided to this reviewer when requested. Five of the questions in the secondary level reading section can be answered from common knowledge without reading the presented material.

Scoring & Interpretation

Manual scoring is simple and quick, except for scoring of the writing sample. It is suggested that the writing sample be judged independently by two persons. A holistic approach, using a scale of 0 to 10 is outlined. It probably requires about three minutes per essay. There are no norms.

Comments

The elementary level of this instrument was designed for students in grades 5-6. Much of the content is common everyday material that would be of average interest to low-income adults and probably not be considered condescending by them. The required reading is at about the 4th grade level. The secondary level of this instrument was designed for students in grades 9-12. Almost all of the content is common everyday material that would be of average interest to low-income adults and probably not be considered condescending. The required reading is at about the 6th grade level.

One 1985 review (in The Ninth Mental Measurements Yearbook, #535) concluded that this instrument measures only a very limited number of very specific skills and only minimal proficiency on them. It adds that these minimal proficiencies are not enough to compete in a technological society. A second review (same source) concluded that a locally prepared minimum proficiency test would work as well because there is nothing new or unique about this instrument.

Reliability of the individual competency scores is so low that the scores should not be used to diagnose individuals or make inferences about their mastery of the individual competencies. This is probably because most of the scores are based on just five items, and that is seldom enough for reliably assessing cognitive skills. The publisher suggests administering both forms of the instrument (Form A and B) so that scores can be based on twice the number of items. This jury-rigged fix is both inconvenient and expensive.

Because of the above comments, this instrument is not well suited to measure the individual competencies it designates. But the various competencies within the reading, writing, and math sections cover a commendable array of skills that would be of use to most adults in their daily life. Since the total reading, writing, and math scores are likely to be more reliable than the competency scores, their use has more merit. Yet they too suffer from a lack of validity and norm data.

Allow longer than normal when ordering materials from this publisher. Both of this reviewer's orders took more than five weeks to arrive, and both were incorrectly filled.

Availability

These instruments are secured and "may be purchased by authorized personnel only." No indication is given of who might qualify for authorization.

Price

 Twenty-five reusable booklets cost $37.50 to $42.50, depending on the level and the section (reading, writing, or math). Fifty answer sheets cost $6.95; one of these answer sheets can be used for all three sections. The manual for the elementary or secondary level costs $3.95. A specimen set for the elementary or secondary level, without the manual, costs $2.50.

Source

IOX Assessment Associates
P.O. Box 24095-W
Los Angeles, CA 90024-0095
(213) 391-6295

Johnston Informal Reading Inventory (JIRI)

Author & Date

Michael C. Johnston

Purpose

To assess the reading comprehension of junior and senior high school students.

Description

This instrument involves a vocabulary screener and several reading passages. The vocabulary part presents 100 words and asks the student to select, from four words following each, the one that means the opposite or almost the opposite of the first. The reading passages are increasingly long and difficult narrative texts. There are passages about a child who finds a hand-grenade and pulls the pin, a swimmer fighting for his life, and an eccentric ice fisherman. After the student has read a passage, he or she returns it and is then given several questions, to which short answers are to be written. The passages start at grade 2 difficulty and extend to grade 10. The questions are about main ideas, details, vocabulary, cause-effect, and inference.

Administration

The instrument can be administered individually or to small groups. Administration is complex in group situations. The vocabulary screener must be administered and scored, and then each student must be given a reading passage at the grade level suggested by his or her vocabulary score. Once the student has finished reading that passage, it must be returned and then the student is given the questions on the passage. When the student has returned the questions and answers for the first passage, he or she is given the passage at the next grade level. This continues until the student scores below 60 percent on two consecutive passages. There is no time limit. Most students complete the vocabulary screener and each of the passages within twenty minutes.

Alternate Forms

There are three forms--Form B, C, and L. The first and second are approximately parallel, and the third in longer.

Reliability

No data on reliability are provided in the manual.

Validity

No data on validity are provided in the manual. There are three unusual features of this instrument that may affect its validity. All the passages are narrative text (stories with characters and action)--none are descriptive, technical, or expository. The questions about the text are given to the student only after he or she has returned the passage. That makes the student's answers a function of both comprehension and memory. The student also must write the answers rather than select among given alternatives. This makes the instrument inappropriate for students who do not write comfortably.

Scoring & Interpretation

Manual scoring is complex and time consuming. The vocabulary part has ten words at each of eight grade levels. The percent correct is to be calculated for each level. It is suggested that the entry level for the reading passages should be two levels below "the highest level of the top three levels in which the student has scored 70% or better on at least two of the three levels." The student's hand-written responses have to be deciphered and compared to the answer key. Some questions can earn more points than others. Partial credit is to be awarded, but there are few guidelines for doing so. For some questions, particularly those about the main idea and inference, there can be more than one good answer, so the scorer has to use judgment. No norm data are reported in the manual.

Comments

This instrument was designed primarily for adolescents. The narrative passages have been selected to be of high interest to such students. They focus on adventure stories, problems of maturing, action sports, and science fiction. Six out of the nine passages in Form B are rural outdoor adventures. They may not be of high interest to most low-income adults.

This instrument is supposed to combine the advantages of individually administered informal reading inventories and group administered instruments. Some might think it does equally well at combining the disadvantages of both.

Availability

The instrument will be sold to anyone.

Price

All three forms of the instrument and the answer key are included in the manual, which costs $9.95. The publisher authorizes duplication of the instrument for classroom use, without obtaining permission.

Source

Educational Publications
532 E. Blackridge
Tucson, AZ 85705

Language Assessment Scales-Reading & Writing (LAS R/W)

Author & Date
Sharon Duncan & Edward De Avila (1987-88)

Purpose
To measure English reading and writing skills of ESL and bilingual education students, especially those skills necessary for functioning in a mainstream academic environment.

Description
Level 1 (for grades 2-3) has six sections measuring reading and writing. Reading is assessed by vocabulary, fluency, mechanics and usage, and reading for information. Writing is assessed by sentence completion and sentence writing. Level 2 (for grade 4-6) has those sections plus one on essay writing. Level 3 (for grades 7-11) has all the sections in Level 2 except the section on sentence completion. All reading items are multiple choice. All the writing items are open-ended and require actual writing.

The vocabulary section has ten items. At Level 1 a picture is presented and the student is to indicate which of four words tells what the picture shows. At Levels 2 and 3 a word is presented and the student is to indicate which of four other words "has the same or about the same meaning." The fluency section has 10 items that measure the ability to infer a missing word based on a knowledge of the language usage and semantics. An example is "Bill wore his _____ to keep his head warm. a) hat b) shoes c) money d) gloves." The mechanics and usage section has 15 items such as "How old are you ___ a) ? b) . c) !" The reading for information section has 10 items. At Level 1 it presents one short narrative and then ten statements that the student is to indicate are "true" or "false" according to the text. At level 3 it presents a multi-paragraph narrative and then ten multiple-choice questions about it. The sentence completion section has five beginnings of sentences and the student is to complete each so that it makes sense, and is warned to write neatly, use good spelling, and pay attention of capitalization and punctuation. The sentence writing section presents five pictures and asks the student to write a sentence about what is happening in each, paying attention to spelling, capitalization, and punctuation. The essay writing section asks the student to write a story about an assigned topic, making sure it has a beginning, middle, and end, is specific and includes details, and uses good spelling, punctuation, capitalization, and paragraph form.

Administration

The instrument may be administered individually or to groups. The instructions are simple and clear. The manual states them only in English, but they are to be given in "whatever language, mixture of languages, or dialects necessary for the student to understand what is required." The instrument items, however, are not to be translated. The instrument is not timed. Most students finish all the reading sections within 55 minutes, and all the writing sections in another 55 minutes.

Alternate Forms

In addition to the three levels indicated above, at each level there are two approximately equivalent forms, Form A and Form B.

Reliability

Test-retest reliability is not reported. Cronbach's Alpha for the section scores has been moderately high (mostly between .70 and .90).

Validity

The total reading and total writing scores on this instrument have correlated moderately highly with comparable scores on the Comprehensive Tests of Basic Skills/Form U (.75 to .91). ESL teachers' judgments of ESL students' oral proficiency has correlated moderately with scores on the LAS. The section scores have low to moderate correlations with each other, indicating that they do measure several fairly distinct skills.

Scoring & Interpretation

Manual scoring of the multiple-choice sections is simple and quick. The sentence completion, sentence writing, and essay writing sections are scored with "focused holistic scoring." The first and second are scored on a scale of 0 to 3 with emphasis on intelligibility, appropriateness to the context of the stimulus, capitalization, punctuation, spelling, and grammar. The essay is scored on a scale of 0 to 5 with emphasis also on transitions, organization, development, and use of vivid and precise vocabulary. The manual provides examples of 0, 1, 2, 3, 4, and 5 responses for each item in the instrument and a brief explanation of why they should be scored as shown. The publisher offers computerized scoring for multiple-choice sections, and scoring of the writing sections by personnel trained in the focused holistic scoring procedures. There are very limited national norm data for majority and minority group elementary and high school students, but norms are not stated in grade levels or percentiles.

Comments

This instrument was developed for elementary and secondary school students. Some of the items are juvenile in content or tone, but many are not.

The reading sections of this instrument look very much like those of common standardized reading achievement tests. Given that the purpose of this instrument is to measure whether minority language students have the English reading skills necessary for functioning in mainstream academic environments, it is not clear why this instrument might serve that purpose better than other commonly used instruments. The writing section makes more use of actual writing samples than most standardized achievement tests. The obvious advantages of that are accompanied by increased complexity in scoring.

Some of the writing stimulus pictures in Level 3 are obscure. The reading for information section has ten items, but all are in reference to a single reading passage. This is not common practice and does not seem advisable, since it is possible for a student to misinterpret an occasional passage despite generally competent reading skills. The mechanics and usage section measures skills that are normally considered part of language usage or writing, rather than part of reading, as this instrument classifies them.

Availability

This instrument will be sold to teachers "in institutions or agencies with signed approval on the CTB/McGraw-Hill order form by his or her administrator." The catalogue says that some instruments require secure handling, but it doesn't indicate which ones.

Price

Thirty-five non-reusable Level 1 student booklets cost $68.25. Thirty-five reusable Level 2 or 3 reading booklets cost $29.05. Thirty-five non-reusable Level 2 or 3 writing booklets cost $35.70. Fifty Level 2 and 3 answer sheets cost $16.00. The manuals for each level cost $6.00 A specimen set, with a copy of the manuals for Levels 1 and 3, costs $12.50. A technical report with reliability and validity data costs $6.00

Source

CTB/McGraw-Hill
2500 Garden Road
Monterey, CA 93940
(800) 538-9547, or (408) 649-8400 from outside the continental United States

Life Skills

Author & Date
Kenneth Majer and Dena Wadell (1977-81)

Purpose
To measure a student's ability to apply reading and math skills to the solution of daily problems

Description
There are two sections, reading and math. The reading section has 48 multiple-choice items that yield four scores: following directions, locating references, gaining information, and understanding forms. The exercises require reading prescription labels, first aid instructions, a catalogue, part of an employee manual, a help wanted ad, a telephone bill, and a consumer loan contract. Most of the items require only literal comprehension--understanding details presented in the reading materials. The math section has 50 multiple-choice items that yield four scores: consumer problems; percentages, interest, and fractional parts; time, currency, and measurement; and graphs, charts, and statistics. The exercises require counting money, totalling bills, computing taxes, calculating simple perimeters and areas, ascertaining elapsed time, converting common measurement units, and reading graphs and charts.

Administration
The instrument can be administered individually or to groups. The instructions are simple and clear. There is no time limit. Most students will finish each section within 40 minutes.

Alternate Forms
There are two parallel forms, Forms 1 and 2.

Reliability
Test-retest reliability, using the two forms administered two weeks apart, was moderately high (.77 for Reading and .79 of Mathematics). KR-20 for the individual competency scores (such as following directions and locating references) have been moderate (mostly .60 to .80). KR-20 for the total reading and total math scores have been high (mostly .90 to .95).

Validity

Neither the manual nor the technical supplement present validity data.

Scoring & Interpretation

One form of the answer sheet has a second sheet in back with carbon in between. The student's marks are transferred to the second sheet which is printed to show which answers are correct. By pulling the two sheets apart, the student or instructor can quickly score the instrument. The regular answer sheets are less expensive, but the publisher does not provide a template for easy manual scoring of them. (A template can be made by marking a sheet of clear acetate.) Computerized scoring is available from the publisher. There are norm data based on 10,000 high school students in 43 schools districts of 24 states. There are additional norm data based on 2,000 inmates of penal institutions in 22 states.

Comments

This instrument was designed to be given to high school students in grades 9-12. But the content is quite adult. The required reading is at about the eighth grade level.

The scores that are produced from this instrument are unusual. In most instruments that measure reading and math, when multiple scores are computed in each skill area, they are usually of component skills such as vocabulary, literal comprehension, and inferential comprehension. In this instrument the scores represent the type of materials used in the exercises, rather than the skills needed in responding. There is nothing inherently wrong with this, but one should be aware of the distinction.

A 1985 review (in The Ninth Mental Measurements Yearbook, #618) concluded that this instrument should not be considered more than a crude first attempt to measure reading and math life skills because of the lack of information in the manuals on how the instrument was developed and validated. Another review (in the same source) concluded that there are at least two other tests that include broader coverage of the full set of life skills competencies; they are the Basic Skills Assessment (reviewed above) and the Competency Testing Program (which apparently is now out of print).

Availability

This instrument will be sold to teachers and school administrators, when the request is on an official purchase order or stationary, and is signed by an appropriate school administrator.

Price

Thirty-five reusable student booklets cost $50.28. Thirty-five self-scoring answer sheets cost $28.74. One Hundred regular answer sheets cost $37.77. The Examiners Manual costs $3.81. The Technical Supplement (manual) costs $15.39. A specimen set costs $4.08.

Source

The Riverside Publishing Company
8420 Bryn Mawr Avenue
Chicago, IL 60631-9979
(808) 323-9540

MAPS Self-Scoring Placement Tests (CGP)

Author & Date

Educational Testing Service (1962-80)

Purpose

To assess reading, writing, and mathematics skills of incoming college students, for purposes of placement.

Description

There are sections on reading, writing, and four levels of mathematics. Each is in separate student booklets.

The reading section asks the student to read eight short passages and answer a total of 35 multiple choice questions about them. There is just one score, the total number correct. The questions are about 1) understanding the main idea ("The passage is mainly about how..."); 2) understanding the secondary idea ("The author sees ... primarily as ... ?"); 3) ability to make inferences ("The ... is welcome because it...?" and 4) understanding vocabulary in context.

The writing section has the student answer 40 multiple choice items. Half of them present a sentence with three words or phrases underlined, and ask the student to indicate whether any of the three are wrong? An example is "Tom <u>ate</u> the hamburger, which <u>was</u> piled high with <u>onions, it</u> was good." The other twenty items present a sentence with a single underlined word or phrase, and ask the student to indicate whether any of three given alternatives is better than the underlined portion, in respect to clarity of ideas, word meaning, and sentence construction and punctuation. There is just one score, the total number correct. The items measure sentence recognition (run-on sentences and incorrect subordinate clauses), sentence structure (parallel structure, dangling modifiers, etc.), pronoun problems (agreement), language and style (distinguishing adverbs from adjectives, distinguishing homonyms, avoiding redundancy), verb problems (agreement and tense), logic (parallelism, distinguishing "but" from "and," cause and effect, etc.), and recognition of error-free construction.

The math sections are on computation, applied arithmetic, elementary algebra, and intermediate algebra. The computation section has 35 multiple-choice items requiring addition, subtraction, multiplication and division of whole numbers, decimals, and fractions; conversions between decimals and fractions; and conversions among different metrics. The applied arithmetic section has 25 multiple-choice word problems that include conversion of metrics, determining unit prices, calculating percents and fractions of a given value, utilizing proportions, calculating a perimeter, totalling a bill, and solving rate/time/quantity problems.

Administration

The instrument can be administered individually or to groups. The instructions are simple and clear. There are time limits of 20 to 25 minutes for each section; some students do not complete all the items.

Alternate Forms

There is only one form of this instrument.

Reliability

Test-retest reliability is not reported in the manual. KR-20 has been high (.83 to.90).

Validity

In many studies, the correlations between the reading and writing scores on this instrument and a first or second semester grade in a college English course have generally been low (.01 to .53, with a medians of .28 and .32, respectively). The correlations between the scores on these instruments and grades in college mathematics courses have generally been moderately low (.06 to .56, with a median of .43). These studies, however, have been mostly in colleges that used the scores on this instrument to place students in appropriate English and math courses. For technical reasons, that won't be explained here, this inevitably reduced the correlations that would have otherwise been found.

Scoring & Interpretation

Manual scoring is easy, quick, and can be done by the students. The answer sheet has carbon on the back and a second sheet behind it indicating the position of the correct answers. After finishing, the student separates the two sheets and counts the number of correct answers. The scoring instructions (printed on the back of the answer sheet) indicate national norms. The norms are based on 30,000 students in 90 2-year and 4-year colleges. Most were community or junior colleges, and few, if any, would be considered to have highly selective admission standards. One-fourth of the students were of minority racial and ethnic groups.

Comments

This instrument was developed for entering college students. The content and tone are adult, but only a few of the passages deal with events and issues common to low-income persons. About fifth grade level reading is required for the math section, about eighth grade level reading is required for the writing section, and the easiest passages in the reading section are at about the eighth grade level.

A 1978 review (in The Eighth Mental Measurements Yearbook, #79) concludes that the evidence of reliability and validity is weak. Better evidence apparently was published after that review, in a manual dated 1979. Other reviews (also in The Eighth

Mental Measurements Yearbook, #7, 61, & 289) generally concluded the instrument can serve its intended purposes.

Availability

This instrument will be sold to anyone.

Price

Twenty-five reusable student booklets for any of the six sections cost $28.75. Twenty-five self-scoring answer sheets cost $23.75. A copy of the manual is provided free with orders for the instrument. A specimen set costs $6.00.

Source

MAPS
CN 6725
Princeton, NJ 08541-6725
(215) 750-8410

McCarthy Individualized Diagnostic Reading Inventory

Author & Date
William G. McCarthy (1971-76)

Purpose
To assess specific reading comprehension and thinking skills.

Description
There are two parts of this instrument. The first part requires the students to read aloud from a word list, read short passages silently and then aloud, and orally answer questions asked by the administrator. The words on the list and the reading passages become progressively more difficult. Performance on the word list is used to determine at which passage the student should start. The reading aloud of each passage is scored in respect to the number of miscues (omissions, substitutions, and insertions) and fluency. If the number of miscues is less than ten, the student is then asked eight comprehension questions. The nature of the questions is the same for all passages. The questions prompt the student to 1) recall a sequence of events, such as, " Did Joe go home before or after Sue?"; 2) recall an exact detail, such as, "What hit the car?"; 3) understand a cause and effect; 4) make up a title that indicates what the passage is about; 5) infer the author's intent, such as, "What do you think the author wanted you to think about?"; 6) evaluate the truth, sensibleness, or reality of a fact or event stated in the passage; 7) judge the mood of the passage; and 8) restate a sentence of the passage with other words. There are grade level scores for oral reading and comprehension, and several other scores.

The second part of the instrument has sections which measure skills in phonics and word analysis; contractions, compound words, and syllables; vocabulary development; sight vocabulary; and study skills.

Administration
The instrument is administered individually. As indicated above, administration is moderately complex. Part 1 is not timed and usually takes 35 to 60 minutes. Part 2 is timed, and takes 34 minutes.

Alternate Forms

There is only one form.

Reliability

The manual states that this instrument is reliable, but presents no data to substantiate that claim.

Validity

The manual states that this instrument is valid, but presents little data to substantiate that claim. The difficulty of the reading passages was determined by use of established readability formulae, however these formulae were not developed to measure the difficulty of the types of comprehension assessed by the questions 4 - 8 for each passage.

Scoring & Interpretation

All the student responses are oral and must be judged by the administrator. The guidelines for doing so are complex and sometimes inconsistent. The fourth through the eighth comprehension questions are not only judged individually, but then again collectively in respect to accuracy of perceptions, willingness to think, organization of thoughts, verbalization of thoughts, willingness to question author, freedom from noticeable bias, and ability to initiate new concepts. Mispronunciations or substitutions, omissions of a word or part of a word, and insertion of words not in the passage, are to be counted as miscues (errors) when scoring the oral reading of the passages. But the directions also state, "Uses of nonstandard or dialect English should not be counted as miscues." Grade level norms are provided for some of the scores, but because of the problem indicated in the section on "Validity" above, there is good reason to question their accuracy.

Comments

The instrument is described by the publisher as suitable for adults as well as elementary school pupils. But the easier reading passages (through the 5th grade level) are distinctly juvenile in content and tone. They may be considered boring or condescending by some adults.

This instrument laudably attempts to assess a broader range of comprehension skills than most reading instruments. But the manner in which it does so, the scoring directions, and the norms appear to be flawed. A 1985 review (in The Ninth Mental Measurements Yearbook, #670) indicated concerns about the skills assessed by this inventory and the manner in which they are measured.

Availability

This instrument is available to everyone.

Price

Reusable student booklets cost $1.60 each. Twelve answer sheets cost $7.50. The administration booklet costs $6.50. The manual (information booklet) costs $2.40. No specimen set is available, but the administration booklet shows all the reading passages and questions asked of the student.

Source

Educators Publishing Service
75 Moulton Street
Cambridge, MA 02238-9101
(800) 225-5750, or (617) 547-6706 within Massachusetts.

Michigan Test of English Language Proficiency (MTELP)

Author & Date

A. Corrigan and others (1961-1979)

Purpose

To measure grammar, vocabulary, and reading comprehension of non-native speakers of English, particularly persons wishing to enroll in colleges and universities where instruction is provided in English.

Description

This instrument has 100 multiple-choice items divided into three parts. Part 1 is comprised of 40 items that measure grammar. Each item presents part of a conversation that includes a short question followed by a short answer. The answer is missing a few words. The student is to select the response choice that is correct grammatically. An example is: "What is that thing? That _____ a spider. a) to call b) for calling c) be called d) is called." Part 2 is comprised of 40 items that measure vocabulary. Some items are a sentence with a missing word, and the student is to select from four response choices the one that best completes the sentence. An example is "Because of the storm and rough waves, it would be foolish to go out sailing today in a small _____. a) automobile b) house c) boat d) beast." Other items are a complete sentence with a single word underlined, and the student is to select from the four response choices the word that means the same thing as the underlined word. Part 3 has four reading passages ranging from 100 to 350 words, and five questions after each. The questions are about details in the passage, arguments made, and conclusions that can be drawn from the passage. The questions generally cannot be answered without reading the passage, even if the student has prior knowledge of the subject matter. Only one score, based on all three sections, is computed.

Administration

The instrument can be administered individually or to groups. The directions for administering the instrument and the instructions for the students are simple and clear. There is a 75 minute time limit.

Alternate Forms

There are seven forms. Forms A, B, D, E, G, and H are secured forms whose distribution is restricted to colleges and universities that use them to screen applicants for admission. Form R is not secured.

Reliability

Test-retest reliability is not reported in the manual. KR-20 and KR-21 have been high (.89 to .92).

Validity

This instrument has had moderate to high correlations (.69 to .90) with the Test of English as a Foreign Language. In a 1956-57 study at one university, the combined score of an early version of this instrument and two others (including the Michigan Test of Aural Comprehension, which is reviewed separately in this handbook) had low to moderate correlations with satisfactory academic performance (.26 to .77) for several different majors. In another study the combined score of the same battery of three instruments had low to high (.10 to .83) correlations with grades earned in several different types of classes.

Scoring & Interpretation

Manual scoring is simple and quick. Norm data are provided. They are based on almost 6,000 persons. The data are reported by native language, but little other information is given about these persons.

Comments

The required reading in Parts 1 and 2 is at about the 6th grade level. Most of the items are about events that are common to all people's lives. At first glance the reading passages appear esoteric. One is on the Doukhobor immigration to Canada and another is about a seventeenth century painter, but if the students keep reading they will find that the former deals with persecution and poverty, and the latter describes a single mother with an unusual career. A 1978 review (in the Eighth Mental Measurements Yearbook #106) concluded this is a well-constructed instrument. It suggested that the instrument should not be used alone as an overall measure of English proficiency, but rather in conjunction with the Michigan Test of Aural Comprehension and a written composition.

Availability

Form R is available to anyone. The other forms are restricted as indicated above in "Alternate Forms."

Price

Twenty reusable student booklets cost $10.00. One hundred answer sheets cost $5.00. The manual costs $2.50. A specimen set, with a copy of the manual, costs $8.00.

Source

ELI Test Publications
English Language Institute
The University of Michigan
Ann Arbor, MI 48109-1057
(313) 747-0456

Minimum Essentials Test
(MET)

Author & Date
William K. Rice and others (1980-81).

Purpose
To measure basic skills and their application to common life situations.

Description
There are scores for reading, language, mathematics, writing, and life skills. There are a total of 125 items. Each section, except that for writing, uses written multiple choice items. The writing section requires the writing of a short essay.

The reading section provides two multi-paragraph passages and asks questions about what the key characters are trying to do, the main idea of a specified paragraph, and the meaning of specified words. The language section asks for the identification of capitalization or punctuation errors, and errors in grammar or sentence structure. The mathematics section consists entirely of computational problems involving addition, subtraction, multiplication, and division of whole numbers, decimals, fractions, and percentages. The writing section requires a one-paragraph essay. The essay is to be about what has happened in a series of three pictures that show a man engaged in a specific task.

The life skills section measures a student's ability to apply reading and basic mathematics to life coping tasks. There are several items in each of the areas of communication, personal finance, employment, health and safety, government and law, and transportation. The items require literal and inferential reading comprehension, quantitative thinking, computation, and problem solving. This section asks the meaning of a common road sign, which of four short letters is the best for a given purpose, what is meant by common instructions on an over-the-counter medication, and several questions about payroll statements, bills, and checkbooks.

Administration
The instrument can be administered to groups or individually. For the reading, language, and mathematics sections, together, there is a time limit of 45 minutes. The writing section requires a one-paragraph essay and there is a 20 minute time limit. The life skills section has a 45 minute time limit. The instructions for administration are simple and clear.

Alternate Forms

The are three forms--A, B, and C. The latter two forms are secured and thus are available only to professional psychologists and evaluators.

Reliability

Test-retest reliability is not reported in the manual. KR-20 coefficients have been high (.84 to .91) for each section of the instrument, except the writing section.

Validity

Data on the validity are not reported in the manual. The reading section has 24 questions, but they are based on just two reading passages and that may adversely affect the validity of the reading score.

Scoring & Interpretation

Manual scoring of the multiple choice items is simple and takes only a few minutes. Computerized scoring by the publisher is also available. National norm data are based on 16,000 students in grades 8 through 12, in 56 school districts across the country.

It is suggested that the writing section be judged holistically by at least two persons. The persons are urged to read the writing sample in its entirety, then immediately judge it as superior, acceptable, marginal, or unacceptable. When the judgments disagree, the writing sample is to be analyzed in respect to four specified criteria.

Comments

This instrument was designed for students in grades 8 to 12 and for adults. Many of the items require reading skills of at least the grade 6 level. A broad array of skills are called for in the life skills section. A 1985 review (The Ninth Mental Measurements Yearbook, #710) indicates that 5 of the 50 life skill items are flawed, resulting in more than one correct answer or no correct answer. Another 1985 review (same source) concluded the instrument should not be used for evaluation purposes until the validity data can be scrutinized.

Availability

The instrument will be sold to individual teachers if the request is on school stationery and countersigned by an administrator.

Price

Thirty-five reusable booklets and one set of directions for administration cost $32.35. Thirty-five answer sheets cost $10.10. The answer key costs $1.70. An instrument review kit costs $9.05

Source

American Testronics
P.O. Box 2270
Iowa City, IA 52244
(800) 553-0030

Objectives-Referenced Bank of Items & Tests (ORBIT)

Author & Date
CTB/McGraw Hill (1975-84)

Purpose
To permit custom developed instruments measuring reading, language arts, mathematics, and social studies.

Description
ORBIT is not a ready-made instrument, rather it is a pool of items designed to measure specific skills. There are items for measuring 357 skills in reading and language arts, 581 skills in mathematics, and 15 skills in social studies. The skills range from those usually taught in kindergarten to those usually taught in 12th grade. Each skill is measured by four multiple-choice items. Skill clusters are defined as a set of 2-4 skills, and are also measured by four multiple-choice items.

The client (an educational institution, an evaluator, etc.) specifies which skills or skill clusters are to be measured, and the publisher uses a computerized typesetting system that efficiently prepares student booklets with just the items that measure those skills. The booklets can have up to 200 items. The order in which the skills are measured is specified by the client. Usually the four items for a given skill or skill cluster are printed on one page, but if graphics are included, they may extend onto a second page.

Administration
The instruments can be administered individually or to groups. Since a multiple-choice
format is used in all the items, standard instructions can be used for any student booklet. The instructions are simple and clear. There is no time limit and most students can finish any item in about one minute.

Alternate Forms
For some skills, there are two or three different sets of items, each set being appropriate for students at different grade levels. But at a given grade level, there is only one set for measuring a given skill.

Reliability

Test-retest reliability in not reported in the manuals. KR-20s have been moderate to high (.73 to .95).

Validity

Technical Bulletin 1 states that validity data are not available.

Scoring & Interpretation

Manual scoring could be easy if a custom scoring template is made on clear acetate. Computerized scoring is available from the publisher. Conventional norm data are not available, but norms can be estimated from a sub-set of items that have been administered to 7,823 elementary and secondary students and which can be included in any custom student booklet. It is not clear how accurate these estimates are.

Comments

The ORBIT system may point the way to the future. It allows the client great latitude in specifying what skills are to be measured, but eliminates the hard work of developing, testing, and refining exercises that measure those skills.

The exercises were developed for elementary and secondary school students. Only a few of the four thousand have been examined by this reviewer. The most elementary ones are juvenile in tone, but the rest were adult in both content and tone. Before using the system in adult literacy programs it might be wise to preview the specific items that are used to measure whatever skills are selected.

The items have been developed by one of the largest measurement organizations in the country, with the assistance of both subject matter experts and measurement experts. But, according to the manuals, many of the items (apparently two-thirds of them) have not been field tested. This is a serious shortcoming. Field testing usually identifies some problems that had not been detected by the experts.

Availability

Custom instruments will be developed with the ORBIT system for teachers "in institutions or agencies with signed approval on the CTB/McGraw-Hill order form by his or her administrator." The catalogue says that some instruments require secure handling, but it doesn't indicate which ones. It takes about 5 weeks to prepare the custom student booklets.

Price

The minimum order is 300 student booklets with 32 items, at a cost of $1,085. Additional items cost $18.00 plus $.015 per student booklet. A specimen set, with a copy of the Buyers Guide and Objectives Book, costs $12.00. Technical Bulletin 1 costs $6.00.

Source

CTB/McGraw-Hill
2500 Garden Road
Monterey, CA 93940
(800) 538-9547, or (408) 649-8400 from outside the continental United States

Official GED Practice Tests

Author & Date
American Council on Education (1987)

Purpose
To help students determine their readiness to take the GED tests.

Description
There are five subtests. They cover writing, social studies, science, interpreting literature and the arts, and mathematics. The GED tests cover the same subjects, but are about twice as long as the practice ones.

The writing skills subtest has two parts. Part 1 has 27 multiple-choice items referencing four passages. Each item repeats a sentence in the passage and then usually asks "What correction should be made to this sentence?" or "Which of the following is the best way to write the underlined portion of this sentence?" The questions focus on language usage, mechanics, and sentence structure. Part 2 asks the students to write an approximately 200-word essay that explains something or presents an opinion in response to a given topic.

The social studies subtest has 32 questions about short passages (a job announcement, legislation, a famous quote, findings of a research study, etc.) and two maps. The passages are about history, geography, economics, political science, and behavioral science. The questions require five kinds of cognitive responses by the students--comprehend the presented material, analyze it, synthesize it, apply it, and evaluate it. Many of the questions can be answered with the information presented and widely common knowledge, but a few require some specialized knowledge that is normally taught in high school. The subtests on science and on interpretation of literature and arts are similar to the social studies subtest.

The mathematics subtest has 28 word problems. They include calculating unit prices, complex bills, and interest on a sum; converting distances on a map to miles of driving; and understanding charts. Simple algebra and geometry are required for answering half of the problems. A full page of formulas that may be needed are provided at the beginning of the section, just as in the GED math test.

72

Administration

The instrument can be administered individually or to groups. The instructions are simple and clear. The time limits for each subtest range from 32.5 minutes to 72.5 minutes.

Alternate Forms

There are two approximately equivalent English forms for use in the U.S., AA and BB. There is also a single Canadian form and a Spanish language form.

Reliability

Test-retest reliability, using the two equivalent U.S. forms, has been high for each subtest (.79 to .86) when assessed with a large sample of high school seniors. The standard errors of estimate ranged from 5.4 to 7.5 units on the standard scale of the full GED tests. KR-20 with a sample of GED candidates was equally high (.81 to .87).

Validity

The subtest scores on the U.S. forms correlated moderately to highly (.66 to .84) with the comparable GED test scores in a large sample of high school students. Validity correlations for GED candidates are not reported.

Scoring & Interpretation

Manual scoring of all but the essay is simple. Scoring of the essay is complex, requires prior training, and is time consuming. An explanation of the procedures and accompanying examples take up 53 pages in the manual. Each essay is to be scored by at least two readers and sometimes three. Even then, the manual warns that these scores are likely to be less reliable than the others. Raw scores are converted to the same standard scale scores as used for the GED tests. The passing scores specified by each state are reported in the manual. The manual also reports the subject area and cognitive skill covered by each multiple-choice item. This can be used to help diagnose particular weaknesses that a student may have.

Comments

This instrument was developed by the same organization that prepares the GED tests, and in accordance with the same specifications used for those tests. The instrument is adult in content and tone. The orientation is generally middle class and academic, but that is appropriate since the same is true of the GED tests.

This is a good predictor of GED test performance--and probably the best available. Because it is not a perfect predictor, however, a student is not reasonably assured of passing in a state that requires all subtests be passed, unless all his or her subtest scores on this practice test are at least 13 points above the minimum pass level.

Though there is no subtest that specifically assesses reading skills, most of this instrument requires considerable reading, at about the 11th grade level. As suggested above, the social studies, science, and literature/arts subtests also require considerable application of critical thinking.

Availability

The instrument will be sold to anyone.

Price

Ten reusable student booklets cost $17.50. Fifty answer sheets cost $9.50. The Teacher's Manual (which is also a technical manual) costs $6.00.

Source

Prentice-Hall
200 Tappan Road
Old Tappan, NJ 07675
(800) 223-1360

Reading Evaluation Adult Diagnosis (Revised) (READ)

Author & Date

Ruth J. Colvin & Jane H. Root (1972-1982)

Purpose

To assess students' reading needs and progress.

Description

The instrument has three parts. The first part assesses sight word recognition--
identifying words without the application of phonic analysis. The student is shown lists
of words and asked to read them aloud. The easiest list includes words like "he" and
"big;" the hardest list includes words like "family" and "arrive." The second part
assesses word analysis--the application of phonics to unfamiliar words. Students are
asked to name the letters of the alphabet, pronounce consonants, and pronounce words
that may be unfamiliar. The third part assesses reading or listening comprehension.
The student is asked to read aloud, and to listen to short passages and answer
questions about them--who, what, where, and how questions.

Administration

This instrument is administered individually. The instructions are sometimes
incomplete and generally complex. The complexity is caused by several factors. These
include: the variety of items, each with different instructions; dividing instructions for a
given exercise among non-contiguous pages; interspersing pre-test and post-test items in
the display materials; and specifying a variety of skip patterns depending on the
student's performance. The administrator is told she may sit beside or across from the
student, but the materials are awkward to use in the first position. In some places the
administrator is told to show a specified list or a subset of a specified list, but the
display materials show several lists on a single page. Apparently the administrator is to
cover the other lists. There is no time limit and no indication of how long the
instrument normally takes to administer.

Alternate Forms

There are two forms of Part 1 and Part 3 of the instrument; there is only one form of
Part 2.

Reliability

No data on reliability are reported in the administrator's manual nor in the supplemental information requested from the publisher.

Validity

No data on validity are reported in the administrator's manual. Supplemental information sent by the publisher indicates that a prior version of this instrument, prepared by a different author, correlated moderately with the reading scores from the Adult Basic Learning Examination. That doesn't say much about this version. The comprehension scores may sometimes be underestimates of silent reading comprehension, since comprehension is assessed only following the student's oral reading to the administrator.

Scoring & Interpretation

Manual scoring is moderately complex, but takes only a few minutes for each administration. No norm data are reported. Implications for instruction are provided in each section of the instrument.

Comments

This instrument is part of the materials used by some of the tutors working with Literacy Volunteers of America. It is intended to be used for diagnosis and monitoring. The reading difficulty ranges up to about grade 5. The short reading passages are generally adult in orientation, but they seem bland and may not be of high interest to most low-income adults.

Availability

This instrument is available to anyone.

Price

One copy of the manual, with the instrument, and one copy of the answer sheet (suitable for administering the instrument twice to the same person) cost $5.50. Additional copies of the answer sheets cost $1.25 apiece.

Source

Literacy Volunteers of America
5795 Widewaters Parkway
Syracuse, NY 13214
(315) 445-8000

Reading/Everyday Activities in Life (R/EAL)

Author & Date
Marilyn Lichtman (1972-1978)

Purpose
To assess capability of reading common everyday print materials.

Description
There are nine reading materials drawn from common everyday print. They include a set of signs, a television program schedule, a recipe, a supermarket newspaper ad, a lease agreement, a road map, classified help-wanted advertisements, and a job application. For some of the materials, the student is given a question and then asked to read the material and provide the answer. For other materials, the student is asked to do the reading first, and then is given the questions. The student is to <u>write</u> the answers in the student booklet. The questions are like: "What do you put in the pan after ...?," "Give one reason mentioned why policemen ...?, and "What is the shortest route shown on the map between A and B?" Very few of the questions require stating the main idea, making inferences, or evaluating the material. There is just one score, the total number of correct answers.

Administration
The instrument can be administered individually or to groups. There is a cassette tape with the directions and comprehension questions. The preferred mode of administration is for each student to have a separate tape recorder with earphones and to proceed at their own pace. The manual indicates, however, that some students may have problems operating the recorder properly. There is no time limit. Most students will finish within 90 minutes. A cassette tape with the instructions in Spanish is also available, but the student booklets with the reading materials are only available in English.

Alternate Forms
There are two forms, Forms A and B.

Reliability
Test-retest reliability is not reported in the manual. KR-20 has been high for Form A (.93), but is not reported for Form B.

Validity

The correlation between Form A of this instrument and the Stanford Achievement Test has been moderately high (.74). Ten of the 45 questions can be answered from common knowledge. Data in the manual indicate that, on the average, the students don't do noticeably better on these ten questions than others, but a few students undoubtedly receive higher scores than they merit because of this shortcoming.

Scoring & Interpretation

The manual lists correct answers for each item, but, as with any open ended questions, there could be other correct ones and the person doing the scoring must use some judgment. Poor handwriting and spelling will make scoring more difficult. Still it is not likely to take more than three minutes per student, especially if the correct answers are retyped in a format that allows easy comparison with the students' answers. It is suggested that a score of 80% correct is required to be considered functionally literate. Limited norm data are provided for 434 "disadvantaged young adults."

Comments

The content and tone are adult. This instrument was designed to measure reading skill in a manner that is as close as possible to everyday reading requirements. It was also designed to be less intimidating to students than conventional reading instruments with multiple-choice responses. For these reasons, the student is presented orally with the comprehension questions and has to construct a response (write it) rather than select from pre-printed multiple-choice responses. There is, however, no evidence in the manual that the instrument is less intimidating. Indeed, students with poor writing skills may be more intimidated by the need to write their responses than they would by the need to select among multiple-choice items (even though errors in spelling and grammar are not counted).

The reading materials and comprehension questions are fairly easy. Fifty percent of disadvantaged youth on whom the norms were calculated answered two-thirds or more of the questions correctly, but the average score of that group on the Stanford Achievement Test was at the grade 5 level.

A 1975 assessment of reading instruments (Tests of Functional Adult Literacy) gave this one a moderately good rating. A 1985 review (in The Ninth Mental Measurements Yearbook, #1034) concluded that the instrument is on the right track, but needs further development.

Availability

This instrument will be sold to anyone.

Price

Non-reusable student booklets cost $1.00 each. The manual costs $6.50. A specimen set, including a copy of the manual, costs $8.00.

Source

Westwood Press
251 Park Avenue South, 14th floor
New York, NY 10010
(212) 420-8008

Slosson Oral Reading Test
(SORT)

Author & Date
Richard L. Slosson (1963)

Purpose
To quickly measure reading skill.

Description
The student is provided with lists of words and asked to "read each word aloud as carefully as you can." There are a total of 200 words. A student will be started at a mid level list if the administrator thinks he or she can do all the words on it, and then directed to an easier list if necessary. There is just one score, the total correct. If a student starts with a mid level list and makes no mistakes, he or she is presumed to have correctly done all the entries on the lower level lists. The words on the easiest list are like: cat, boy, and work. The words on the hardest list are like: glaze, invincible, and repression.

Administration
The instrument must be individually administered. The instructions are simple and clear. There is no time limit, but only five seconds are permitted for pronunciation of each word. Most students finish within five minutes.

Alternate Forms
There are two forms, SIT-3A for students in elementary and secondary school, and SIT-3AB for students in adult literacy programs and the visually and verbally handicapped. Both use the same word list, but the latter uses larger print and modified instructions to establish rapport with adults.

Reliability
The publisher's catalog indicates that test-retest reliability has been very high (.99) after one week. That value is suspiciously high; it may be a result of chance or a computational error.

Validity
The publisher's catalog says that the score of this instrument has correlated very highly (.96) with the score on the Standardized Oral Reading Paragraphs. No correlations with silent reading instruments are reported.

Scoring & Interpretation

Scoring is simple and quick. A pause of more than five seconds or a mispronunciation is counted as an error. Norm data are presented, indicating grade levels for various total scores. The publisher's material, copyrighted in 1963, says that "The words have been taken from standardized school readers and the Reading Level obtained from testing represents median or standardized school achievement." That doesn't say much about how the norms were developed, and no further details are given. All the words are still in common use, but the more difficult lists appear to be at about one grade level above what is indicated in the norms.

Comments

This instrument was designed for elementary and secondary school pupils. The words on the two easiest lists tend to be juvenile, but the rest of the lists are comprised of words commonly used by adults. The main advantages of the instrument are that it can be used with very low level readers and it is quick and easy to administer.

The instrument is old, and shows its age. Newer reading tests focus on silent reading, since it is more important to most people than reading aloud. Several practitioners in adult literacy have noted that some adults are better at reading words in the context of a sentence than in isolation, as is the case with word lists.

The publisher does not sell a manual for this instrument and provides only limited information about it. The amount of information is less than required by current professional standards.

The standard instrument has all the lists on one page of paper. This could be distracting and anxiety-producing to the student, as he or she might glance at the words still to come. The instrument is also available on flipcards, with just one list on each card.

Availability

The instrument is sold to teachers, counselors, and school administrators. Orders must state the purchaser's profession and be signed by authorized personnel.

Price

Fifty copies of the instrument cost $9.00. There is no separate answer sheet and no manual. The publisher will mail a single copy of the instrument, for examination, without charge.

Source

Slosson Educational Publications
P.O. Box 280
East Aurora, NY 14052
(800) 828-4800, or (716) 652-0930 within New York

Spanish Assessment of Basic Education (SABE)

Author & Date
CTB/McGraw Hill (1987)

Purpose
To assess basic reading and mathematics skills commonly taught to U.S. students for whom Spanish is the language of instruction.

Description
This instrument yields scores for word attack, vocabulary, reading comprehension, mathematics computation, and mathematics concepts and applications. There are 126 to 175 items, depending on the level of the instrument. All the instructions for the students and all the exercises are in Spanish. The manual for the administrator is in English.

Administration
The instrument can be administered individually or to groups. The instructions are simple and clear. There are time limits, but they have been selected so that most students will complete each section. Administration takes about two and a half hours.

Alternate Forms
There is one form at each of six levels. The levels span grades 1 to 8. There also is a practice instrument for each level, which acquaints the students with the format of the questions and the manner of marking the answers.

Reliability
The technical report had not been published at the time of this review.

Validity
The technical report had not been published at the time of this review.

Scoring & Interpretation
Manual scoring is simple, but takes a couple of minutes per instrument because of the large number of items. Computerized scoring is available from the publisher. There are norm data from 8,000 elementary and Junior high school Spanish-speaking students in maintenance and transitional bilingual programs throughout the U.S. The scores can

also be equated with the Comprehensive Tests of Basic Skills and the California Achievement Tests.

Comments

This is a new instrument, resulting from a major development effort. It was prepared specifically for Spanish-dominant elementary and Junior high school students. The content and language were selected to be appropriate to them.

Availability

The instrument will be sold to teachers "in institutions or agencies with signed approval on the CTB order form of his or her administrator." The catalogue says that some instruments require secure handling, but it doesn't indicate which ones.

Price

Thirty-five non-reusable booklets for Levels 1, 2, or 3 cost $45.85-$64.40. Thirty-five reusable booklets for Levels 4, 5, or 6 cost $45.85. Fifty answer sheets for Levels 4-6 cost $15.50. One hundred practice instruments for Levels 1, 2-3, or 4-6 cost $5.25. A multi-level review kit, including the examiner's manual and norms book, but not the technical report, costs $28.25. The technical report costs $7.55.

Source

Publishers Test Service
CTB/McGraw-Hill
2500 Garden Road
Monterey, CA 93940
(800) 538-9547, or (408) 649-8400 from outside the continental United States

Spanish/English Reading Comprehension Test

Author & Date
Steve Moreno (1978)

Purpose
To assess reading skills in Spanish and English, particularly the relative skill in both.

Description
This instrument was originally developed and normed in Mexico, and based on curriculum materials commonly used in that country. The English version was translated from the Spanish version and then normed in the United States. In the Spanish version, both the instructions given to the students and the exercises are in Spanish. There are 71 or 81 items, depending of the level used. There is only one score, the total number of correctly answered questions. All but a few items involve answering multiple-choice questions about short reading passages. Most of the questions are about details presented in the passages. There are questions like: "What color was the car? a) red, b) green c) yellow d) black;" and, "The boy was: a) happy b) scared c) curious d) sad."

Administration
This instrument can be administered individually or to a group. The instructions are simple and clear. There is a 25 minute time limit.

Alternate Forms
There are two forms, Spanish and English. There are two levels of each of those forms, one for grades 1 to 6, and one for grades 7 to 12 plus adults.

Reliability
Test-retest validity is not reported in the manual. For the Spanish form, the split-half reliability has been high (.88 to .94).

Validity
For the Spanish form, the scores have correlated moderately (.48 to .65) with teachers' rankings of their students' reading ability. For several of the questions, some of the response choices can be eliminated by use of common knowledge without reading the passage. This can adversely affect the validity of the scores.

Scoring & Interpretation

Manual scoring is simple and quick. The norms for the upper level of the Spanish form are based on about 3,000 urban and rural high school students in six states of Mexico. The norms for the upper level of the English form are based on about 2,000 American high school students in six states; all were fluent English speakers.

Comments

The lower level (grades 1 to 6) of this instrument is distinctly juvenile in content and tone. Some adults would probably find it uninteresting or condescending. The higher level (grades 7 to 12, and adults) has more mature content, but nine of the 15 passages are about children, adolescents, or mythology.

A 1985 review (in The Ninth Mental Measurements Yearbook #1161) suggests that neither the Spanish or English form should be used in this country because they are based on the curriculum, localisms, and dialects of Mexico. That review also states there is little evidence that the Spanish and English version are equivalent for measurement purposes. (Translations are not always of equivalent reading difficulty.) A second review (in the same source) concluded that the instrument has promise, but additional reliability and validity studies are needed.

Some of the language in the English version is a bit stilted, apparently as a result of the translation from the Spanish original. Two of the passages in the higher level of the instrument are filled with Indian names that might be difficult for native English speakers. Otherwise the English form looks much like many reading instruments developed in this country.

This instrument mainly assesses literal comprehension. Almost all the questions are about details presented in the passages. There are few, if any, questions requiring summarization of the passages, inferences, or evaluation.

Availability

The instrument should be administered by teachers, psychologists, or other certified professionals.

Price

Non-reusable student booklets cost $0.35 apiece. The manual costs $11.00.

Source

Moreno Educational Company
7050 Belle Glade Lane
San Diego, CA 92119
(619) 461-0565

SRA Reading and Arithmetic Indexes

Author & Date
Science Research Associates (1968-86)

Purpose
To measure general reading and math computation skills, particularly of applicants for entry-level jobs and job training programs.

Description
The reading and math sections are in separate booklets. The reading section has 60 multiple-choice items that require the student to: select one of four words that is represented by a given picture; complete a phrase with one of four words that have similar beginnings, but different endings (such as, "A cook makes a) sugar b) salad c) sand d) salt); complete a phrase with one of four phrases ending in the same word; select one of four sentences that means the same thing as a given one; and answer questions about short paragraphs. Most items require only literal comprehension. The arithmetic section has 60 multiple choice items that require basic computations with whole numbers, fractions, and decimals, and percentages. There are no word problems.

Administration
The instrument can be administered individually or to groups. The instructions are simple and clear. There is no time limit; most students finish each section within 25 minutes.

Alternate Forms
There is just one form.

Reliability
Test-retest reliability is not reported in the manual. KR-20 reliability has been high (.87 to .95).

Validity
The manual does not report correlations between the reading score and other measures of reading. The arithmetic score has correlated moderately with the FIT Arithmetic score (.55 to .68). The reading and arithmetic scores have generally had low correlations (.00 to .32) with job performance.

Scoring & Interpretation

Manual scoring is moderately simple and takes a few minutes for each section. The student marks his or her answers in the student booklet. Each page has carbon paper on the back that transfers the student's marks to a form that shows which answers are correct. When the carbon paper is torn out, the marks on the form are visible. The items within the reading and arithmetic sections are clustered according to several levels of difficult, and each is scored separately. Pass scores for each level are used to determine at which level the student is performing. The reading levels are: 1) picture-word associations, 2) word decoding, 3) phrase comprehension, 4) sentence comprehension, and 5) paragraph comprehension. The arithmetic levels are: 1) addition and subtraction of whole numbers, 2) multiplication and division of whole numbers, 3) addition, subtraction, multiplication and division of fractions, and 4) addition, subtraction, multiplication and division of decimals and percentages. Approximate grade equivalents of each of these levels are reported. Limited norm data are given for 57 job trainees in one Chicago program, 419 students in Colorado and South Carolina special education and adult education classes, and more than 2,000 employees in a variety of occupations. The latter are reported separately by occupational clusters.

Comments

This instrument was developed for adolescents and adults. The content and tone is adult. The instrument received mediocre ratings in a 1975 analysis (Tests of Functional Adult Literacy). Most of the reading section requires only low and intermediate levels of reading. Half of the unskilled workers taking it missed less than seven of the 60 items. The arithmetic section is somewhat more difficult.

This reviewer has substantial experience administering the reading section to low and intermediate level literacy students. He is generally pleased with how it has worked. The first 19 items have very simple formats and require only a low level of reading. That allows all but the totally illiterate to get off to a good start. Students do not seem offended by the instrument, they apply themselves and persevere, and they often perform somewhat better than their teachers expected. There is, however, a problem with the last half of the instrument. It requires reading at grades 6-9, and low level readers will find the passages impossibly difficult. Some students have felt frustrated at not being able to finish, but other students with similar skills have expressed surprise and pride in being able to make it even half-way through the booklet. The directions to the students given in the manual should probably be supplemented with a statement that forewarns of the increasing difficulty, encourages the students to do the best they can, and suggests that when the items get too difficult they should go back and recheck their answers to the earlier questions.

Availability

This instrument will be sold to personnel in businesses, associations, or other institutions having legitimate need for assessment instruments and using them in a secure and professional manner.

Price

Twenty-five self-scoring non-reusable student booklets of either the reading or arithmetic section cost $21.00. The manual costs $10.00. The product manager can be reached at (312) 984-7016.

Source

Science Research Associates
P.O. Box 5380
Chicago, IL 60680-5380
(800) 772-1277, or (312) 984-7000 within Illinois.

Test of Written Language (TOWL)

Author & Date
Donald D. Hammil & Stephen Larsen (1978-83)

Purpose
To measure skill in written expression.

Description
This instrument has four parts. The first part presents sentences with one missing word and asks the student to fill in the proper word. This part is to measure word usage--selection of suitable words, proper tenses of verbs, appropriate cases of pronouns, and proper subject-verb agreement. The second part presents three fictional pictures and directs the student to "make up a good story to go with them." This is to measure thematic maturity, vocabulary, and handwriting. The third part asks the student to write down words--spelling them correctly--as they are dictated. The fourth asks the student to rewrite, with correct punctuation and capitalization, sentences presented without any punctuation and capitalization. There are seven scores: word usage, thematic maturity, vocabulary, handwriting, spelling, style, and total competence.

Administration
The instrument can be administered individually or to groups. The instructions are simple and clear, but are missing important information. The instructions to the students for completing the sentences merely say "fill in the missing word." There is no direction indicating the choice should comply with the rules for standard English. No purpose or criteria are specified for the story to be written by the student. Students are not told to write neatly, but handwriting is scored; students are not told to use large words, but that is scored; and students are not told to make it a long story, but length increases the likely score. There is no time limit, but the spelling section is paced because the student is to write dictated words. Most students finish the instrument within 40 minutes.

Alternate Forms

There is only one form.

Reliability

Test-retest reliability has been moderate to high (.68 to .99) except for the vocabulary score in elementary grades (.38 to .56). Split-half reliability has been high (.80 to .96) for the style, spelling, and word usages scores. It can't be computed for the other scores. Inter-scorer agreement in the scoring of the stories written by the students has been moderate to high (.76 to .98).

Validity

Correlations between this instrument's scores and those of several other measures have generally been low to moderate (mostly between .30 and .70). The other measures have included the Picture Story Language Test, The Test of Adolescent Language, and the Language score of the Comprehensive Test of Basic Skills. The manual indicates that the spelling and word usage parts of the instrument are too easy to be valid for high school students.

Scoring & Interpretation

Scoring is moderately difficult and time-consuming. For the incomplete sentences, there can be more than one correct answer. The manual gives examples of common correct and incorrect responses, but there could be others. The story the student writes is judged for thematic maturity, vocabulary, and handwriting. Thematic maturity is scored by assigning points for each of twenty features which it incorporates, including giving personal names to the main characters, making the story part of a dream sequence, and expressing some philosophical or moral theme. The manual provides several sample stories, showing them without scoring and then scored with annotations. Vocabulary is scored by giving one point for each word of seven characters or more in length, except for specified exceptions. Handwriting is to be rated in comparison to five samples shown in the manual. National norm data, by student age, are reported in the manual. They are based on 3,418 students, age 7 to 19, in all regions of the country.

Comments

This instrument was developed for elementary and secondary students. The content and tone are juvenile, and some adults may find the instrument condescending or boring.

A reading level of about the fifth grade level is required. One 1985 review (in The Ninth Mental Measurements Yearbook, #1278) concluded that the instrument is one of the best currently available for evaluating written language. Another review, in the same source, described it as an important new direction in assessing written language.

Availability

This instrument is sold to anyone.

Price

Fifty non-reusable student booklets cost $21.00. The manual costs $24.00. A specimen set, including a copy of the manual, costs $24.00.

Source

PRO-ED
5341 Industrial Oaks Blvd.
Austin, TX 78735
(512) 892-3142

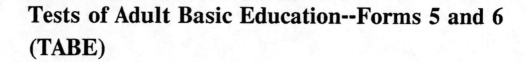

Tests of Adult Basic Education--Forms 5 and 6 (TABE)

Author & Date
CTB/McGraw Hill (1957-1987)

Purpose
To measure reading, writing, and math achievement.

Description
The complete version of this instrument has seven sections with a total of 263 multiple-choice items. The vocabulary section has four types of items: choosing a word that has the same meaning or opposite meaning as a given word; choosing a word that has the same meanings as two given phrases (example: "a season and to jump: a) fall b) dart c) spring d) leap"); indicating the meaning of a prefix or suffix; and choosing a word that is appropriate for a blank in a given sentence. The reading comprehension section has short reading passages followed by questions on word meaning, details, main ideas, tone, conclusions, and inferences. The language mechanics section covers the use of capitalization and punctuation. The language expression section focuses on usage, sentence structure, and paragraph development. It requires choosing a word or phrase that best fits in the blank of a given sentence; combining two sentences into one; selecting a leading topic sentence that best fits a given paragraph; choosing a brief paragraph that best fits a leading topic sentence; editing out a sentence that does not fit in a given paragraph; and ordering given sentences into a paragraph. The spelling section requires choosing among given spelling variants the word that best fits in the blank of a given sentence. The mathematical calculation section requires adding, subtracting, multiplying, and dividing whole numbers, decimals, fractions, and percents. The section on mathematical concepts and applications has a broad range of word problems including the conversion of metrics, the interpretation of charts and graphs, time/rate/quantity problems, identification of basic geometric concepts, computation of volumes of simple geometric shapes, and solving simple algebraic equations.

Administration
The TABE can be administered individually or to groups. Administration is moderately simple. A brief screener of reading and mathematics is given to determine which level instruments the student should receive. The reading score on the screener is used to assign the appropriate level of the reading, language and spelling sections to each student. The math score on the screener is used to assign the appropriate level of the math sections. There is a time limit for each section. The manual claims that ninety percent of the students can answer all the items that they know within the time

limits, but this reviewer suspects the actual percentage is lower. The total time for all seven sections is 3.3 hours. The instructions given by the administrator are the same for all four levels of each section, thus permitting simultaneous administration of different levels to a given group of students.

Alternate Forms

There is a screener (Locator), four different levels of a short version (Survey Form), and four levels and two equivalent forms of the long version (Complete Battery--Forms
5 and 6). The levels correspond in difficulty to grades: 2-4, 4-6, 6-8, and 8-12.

Reliability

Test-retest reliability is not reported in the manuals. KR-20 reliability has been high (mostly .80 to .90).

Validity

Limited validity data are reported in the manuals. The scores on the TABE have correlated moderately (.55 to .64) with comparable scores on the GED.

Scoring & Interpretation

Manual scoring is moderately easy, but takes a few minutes for each student because of the large number of items and the seven sections. The number correct on each section is converted to a scale score, percentile, or grade equivalent by looking in the appropriate norm tables. Computerized scoring is available. The norm data are based on 6,300 students in 223 institutions across the country. Norms are reported separately for adult basic education students, adult offenders, juvenile offenders, and vocational/technical school enrolles. About two-thirds were minority. Norm data also permit prediction of GED scores. Scores on the new (1986) instrument can be equated with those of the prior version (1976--Forms 3 and 4).

Comments

The TABE is one of the most widely used instruments in adult education programs. It was thoroughly revised in 1986. All the items are new, the range of skill levels that can be assessed has been extended, and the specific skills that are measured has been more finely divided and identified.

This instrument was designed for adults. Though the items are adult in content, they seem distinctly middle class and academic in orientation. Only a modest portion of them are about everyday events in low-income adults' lives. For instance, in the grade 4-6 level booklet (Form 5M), only two of the eight reading passages are about experiences common to such students. Of the 40 items on math concepts and application there is only one item on calculating the correct change for a given transaction, no item on the savings from bulk purchases, and no item on the total cost of a purchase with installment plan financing charges.

This instrument assesses an unusually large number of skills within reading and writing. The language mechanics and expression sections are notable for focusing not only on sentence construction, but also paragraph construction. There is, however, no provision for judging writing samples generated by the student.

The lowest level of the TABE requires reading skills equal to about the end of the second grade, and thus it is not appropriate for beginning readers.

Availability

The instrument will be sold to teachers "in institutions or agencies with signed approval on the CTB order form of his or her administrator." This is a secured instrument and must be treated appropriately.

Price

Twenty-five reusable screener booklets cost $16.75. Twenty-five reusable student booklets with the reading, math, and language instruments together, cost $33.50. Note that these booklets are sold in lots of 25, for each of four levels of difficulty; if three levels of difficulty are needed, 75 booklets must be purchased. Fifty answer sheets cost $8.50 to $16.70, depending on which of four types are ordered. The Examiner's Manual costs $5.25; the Norms Book costs $5.35; the Test Coordinator's Handbook costs $7.55; and the Technical Report costs $7.55. A specimen set, with a copy of the Examiner's manual but not the Norms Book or Technical Report, costs $10.80.

Source

Publishers Test Service
CTB/McGraw-Hill
2500 Garden Road
Monterey, CA 93940
(800) 538-9547, or (408) 649-8400 from outside the continental United States

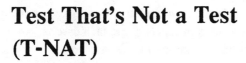

Test That's Not a Test
(T-NAT)

Author & Date
Don Brown (1974)

Purpose
To screen for reading ability in a manner that does not seem like a test.

Description
There are six cards that are to be read aloud by the student. Each is a short description or story. The first card has three short sentences describing a man named Bill; the reading difficulty is about at the first grade level. The sixth card has an eight-sentence story describing a man who thinks he is having a heart attack; the reading difficulty is about at the sixth grade level. There is one score, a grade level estimate based on the highest numbered card that the student reads successfully. Six types of errors are counted: mispronunciations (but not dialect variations), substitutions (saying an entirely different word), omissions, additions, words the student hesitates on and can't pronounce, and transpositions in word order.

Administration
The instrument must be administered individually, but to do so is simple and quick. The instructions to the student are simple and clear. There is no time limit. Most students should finish within ten minutes. The administrator is told, "all appearance of a formal testing situation is to be avoided."

Alternate Forms
There are two forms, one for elementary and secondary students and one for adults. The specimen sent to this reviewer had no indication of its form. It starts with stories titled "Bill" and "Shopping" and appears to be the adult form.

Reliability
No reliability data were sent by the publisher, and the price list does not indicate any supplemental materials that are likely to include this information. Because the administration is terminated after a student does not successfully read one or two cards, reliability will probably not be high for students reading at grades 1-3.

Validity

No validity data were sent by the publisher, and the price list does not indicate any supplemental materials that are likely to include this information.

Scoring & Interpretation

Scoring is quick and fairly simple. The administrator is to keep a count of the number of errors in his or her head. That is practical since each card is scored separately and none should take the student more than two minutes to read. If the student makes more errors than the number of the card, the grade level corresponding with that number has not been achieved.

Comments

This instrument is adult in content and tone. It makes an effort to eliminate the appearances of testing. There also is no use of stop-watches, scoring sheets, and clip-boards. Reading short paragraphs may appear less like a test to adults than reading word lists. Never-the-less, reading aloud to an authority figure may seem artificial and test-like to many adults.

Availability

The instrument will be sold to anyone.

Price

A complete kit, with a reusable set of reading cards and instructions for administration and scoring, costs $7.95. There is no separate manual.

Source

Basic Education Trade House
P.O. Box 3102
Greeley, CO 80633-3102
(303) 351-0791

Wide Range Achievement Test
(WRAT-R)

Author & Date
Sarah Jastak and Gary S. Wilkinson (1936-1984)

Purpose
To quickly assess skill in reading, spelling and arithmetic for persons aged 5 to 75.

Description
There are three scores--for reading, spelling, and arithmetic. The reading section involves recognizing and naming letters and pronouncing words on a list. There are 89 to 100 items, depending on the level of the instrument used. The spelling section involves copying marks that resemble letters, writing single words that are dictated, and writing one's name. There are 51 - 65 items. The arithmetic section involves counting, reading number symbols, solving orally presented computational problems, and doing written computations. Level R2 includes power and square root functions; logs; and algebraic operations. There are 59 - 66 items.

Administration
The instrument is usually administered individually, but the spelling and arithmetic sections can be administered to groups of adults. Administration is moderately complex. For instance, in the reading section, students are to be given only ten seconds to pronounce each word on the oral reading lists; the testing is to be terminated after 10 consecutive errors; and if the student earns a score of less than 10 when reading words aloud, he or she is then to be given several pre-reading items. The directions to the administrator are occasionally awkward, inconsistent, or incomplete.

The instructions to the student are clear and simple. The administration is usually paced and there is a fixed time limit (10 minutes) for the arithmetic section. Administration of the full instrument usually takes 20 - 30 minutes.

Alternate Forms
There are two levels. Level R1 is for ages 5 through 11; level R2 is for ages 12 through 75. There is only one form at each level.

Reliability

Test-retest reliability has been high for each of the three scores (.79 to .97). Internal consistency, measured by person and item separation coefficients, has generally been high (mostly between .84 and .99).

Validity

The average scores for the norm data increase for almost each successive age group through early adulthood. The scores correlate moderately or highly with comparable scores on the California Achievement Test, the Stanford Achievement Test, and other achievement batteries (mostly .66 to .85).

Scoring & Interpretation

Manual scoring is moderately complex, but takes less than five minutes. The complexity is caused by the need to decide whether the words read aloud were pronounced correctly, by the need to decipher the student's handwriting in the spelling section, and because not all items are given one point if answered correctly. There are norm data from a national sample of 5600 persons. Norms are reported for 28 different age groups. Grade equivalents are also provided.

Comments

The WRAT is one of the longest lived measures of basic skills. Despite several revisions, its age is apparent.

Modern instruments do not measure reading only by the pronunciation of words on lists. Modern math instruments don't measure math skills without word problems.

The manual states that, "The WRAT-R was intentionally designed to eliminate, as totally as possible, the effects of comprehension." For diagnostic purposes, the authors wanted to assess only decoding and computational skills, and they felt that performance on comprehension and problem solving tasks is a function of intelligence as well as these skills. This narrow focus of the WRAT can be useful for some diagnostic purposes. But it makes the instrument inappropriate for assessing student's skill in real-life applications of reading and math. Level R2 of this instrument was designed for people from age 13 and up. Some adults will probably find the exercises condescending, but the quick, individual administration is likely to make that not much of a problem. The reading and arithmetic items in the adult level (R2) quickly become difficult. Most students in beginning level literacy programs will be struggling before they get one-third the way through. The R1 level of the instrument will be less frustrating and a more accurate measure of their skills. It's format and tone are almost identical with that of level R2.

One 1985 review (in The Ninth Mental Measurements Yearbook, #1364) concluded this instrument offers little as a measure of achievement, but another review (same source) said it is adequate for assessing the three areas it covers.

Availability

The instrument will be sold to teachers "in institutions or agencies with signed approval on the CTB order form of his or her administrator." The catalogue says that some instruments require secure handling, but it doesn't indicate which ones.

Price

Twenty-five copies of the answer sheet for either level of the instrument cost $10.00. The Manual costs $23.00

Source

Publishers Test Service
CTB/McGraw-Hill
2500 Garden Road
Monterey, CA 93940
(800) 538-9547, or (408) 649-8400 from outside the continental United States

Woodcock-Johnson Psycho-Educational Battery

Author & Date

Richard W. Woodcock and Mary B. Johnson (1977-1978).

Purpose

To measure cognitive ability, scholastic aptitude, academic achievement, and academic interests.

Description

This is a battery of instruments assessing each of the characteristics indicated immediately above. The academic achievement section measures reading, math, and written language. The reading part focuses on letter-word identification, word attack, and passage comprehension. The math part focuses on computations and applied problems. The written language part focuses on dictation and proofing.

Administration

The instruments must be individually administered. The procedure is moderately complex and the instructions to the students are mediocre. It takes two hours to administer the full set of instruments.

Alternate Forms

There is a Spanish version of 17 of the 27 sections.

Reliability

Test-retest reliability of the section scores is high (.83 to .97).

Validity

The achievement scores correlate moderately or highly (.70 to .90) with the Peabody Picture Vocabulary Test and the Wide Range Achievement Test.

Scoring & Interpretation

Manual scoring is arduous and time consuming. Computerized scoring is available from the publisher. There are national norm data for the English version based on 4,732 persons; and norm data for the Spanish version are based on 802 persons from five Spanish speaking countries.

Comments

The information in this review is based only on the publisher's catalogue and other published reviews. The publisher does not offer a specimen set. To examine the achievement instrument and instructions for its use would have cost $94.50.

This battery of instruments was developed for use with persons from age 3 to 80. A 1985 review (in the Ninth Mental Measurements Yearbook, #1387) concluded that this instrument is a well developed one and "the achievement section provides a more comprehensive measure of reading, written language, ...[and] mathematics... than any of the present individually administered survey instruments." A second 1985 review (in the same source) praised the originality of the exercises, the technical expertise manifest in the development of the instrument, and its reliability and validity, but criticized the complexity in generating and interpreting the scores.

Availability

Orders from individual teachers must be approved by the appropriate school administrator. For non-accredited schools, there must be evidence that the person responsible for the instrument is qualified by training or experience to professionally administer such instruments.

Price

A set of materials for administering the achievement instruments to 25 students costs $84.00. The examiner's manual costs another $10.50. Twenty-five additional answer booklets cost $20.00.

Source

DLM Teaching Resources
P.O. Box 4000
Allen, TX 75002
(800) 527-4747, or (800) 442-4711 in Texas

Oral English
Proficiency
of ESL Students

Introduction

Oral language skills include both listening and speaking. Within each of these there is a vast variety of skills and range of proficiency, including phonic discrimination, vocabulary, pronunciation, grammar, idioms, organization, and utilization of contextual clues.

The instruments reviewed in this section include some that focus on rudimentary oral language, some that focus on intermediate proficiency, and some that assess whether a student is prepared to handle college instruction in English. Many cover both listening and speaking skills, but a few cover just one or the other.

Almost all of the instruments that focus on rudimentary and intermediate proficiency must be administered to students individually. That makes them much more time-consuming to use than most instruments listed in the other sections of this book.

Instruments that Measure Oral English Proficiency

Instrument	Page	Reading requirements
Basic English Skills Test (BEST)	107	No reading for most items
Bilingual Vocational Oral Proficiency Test (BVOPT)	110	No reading
CASAS Adult Life Skills Language Tests	113	Levels A and B require no reading; Level C requires at least Grade 5 reading
English as a Second Language Oral Assessment (ESLOA)	116	No reading
The John Test / The Fred Test	118	No reading
Language Assessment Scales--Oral (LAS-O)	121	No reading
Language Facility Test (LFT)	124	No reading
Listening Comprehension Test (LCT)	126	At least Grade 4 reading
Michigan Test of Aural Comprehension (MTAC)	128	At least Grade 4 reading
Oral English/Spanish Proficiency	130	No reading
Secondary Level English Proficiency Test (SLEP)	132	At least Grade 4 reading
The Second Language Oral Test of English (SLOTE)	134	No reading
Test of English as a Foreign Language (TOEFL)	137	At least Grade 6 reading

Basic English Skills Test
(BEST)

Author & Date

Center for Applied Linguistics (1981-1987)

Purpose

To assess speaking, listening, reading, and writing skills of low proficiency non-native English speakers.

Description

There are two sections. The first section has 50 items and yields five scores for listening comprehension, pronunciation, communication, fluency, and reading/writing. This section is mostly an oral interview that asks several personal questions and then asks questions and gives the students directions to follow in response to photographs, signs, a map, and some money placed on the table. The questions ask what the people are doing in the pictures, where a specified object is (the student is to point to it), what a given sign means, and what time is shown by given clocks. The directions are to move one's finger on a map as directed and to select a specified amount of money from a small pile on the desk. A few reading and writing items are included. The second section assesses reading and writing skills more thoroughly.

Administration

The first section must be administered individually and to do so is moderately simple. A few questions are to be skipped or have their wording modified, depending on a prior response. The administration is paced and takes about 10 to 20 minutes. The second section can be administered individually or to groups. It has a time limit of one hour.

Alternate Forms

There is only one level. Two forms, Forms B and C are currently available. The latter was just recently released.

Reliability

Test-retest reliability is not reported in the manual. KR-20 has been moderately high (.78 to .86) for the listening, communication, and fluency scores, and high (.91) for the total of the oral interview section. Inter-rater reliability, which is important when the scoring is judgmental, has also been high (.84 to .98) after careful training.

Validity

Students assigned to seven ESL instructional levels by means other than the BEST instrument, were administered the BEST and the mean score of students was substantially higher in each successive level.

Scoring & Interpretation

Most of the scoring of the first section is done while it is administered, rather than later from a tape recording. That saves time, but it can be distracting to the student and sometimes to the administrator. The scoring is judgmental and moderately complex. Listening comprehension items are scored as demonstrating comprehension or not. Communi- cation items are scored as comprehensible and grammatically accurate; comprehensible, but not grammatically accurate; and not comprehensible, or comprehensible but inappropriate. Fluency items are scored as conveying much information and detail, conveying a moderate amount of information and detail, terse, and no response or an incomprehensible one. Pronunciation is not measured by specific items, but rather is based on the student's speech throughout the interview; it is scored as readily understandable, generally understandable, or frequently not understandable.

The oral interview total score does not include the pronunciation score, and no reason is given in the manual for that. Though the instrument was administered to 987 ESL students during its refinement, no norm data are reported in the manual. The manual does describe "Student Performance Levels" for various total scores, but the basis for the specified levels is not given.

Comments

This instrument was developed for adults and is appropriate for them in content and tone. A recent review of the instrument (in Reviews of English Language Proficiency Tests, page 10) described it as exciting, innovative, and valid, but time-consuming to use and lacking justification for the scoring system.

Availability

This instrument will be sold to anyone who signs the publisher's agreement specifying appropriate practices for its use.

Price

The picture book to which the student responds in the first section of the instrument costs $9.00. Five copies of the administrator's interview guide for that section cost $10.00. One hundred scoring sheets for that section cost $20.00. Twenty student booklets and scoring sheets for the second section cost $40.00. The manual costs $15.00. A specimen set, without a copy of the manual, is free.

Source

Center for Applied Linguistics
1118 22nd Street N.W.
Washington, DC 20037
(202) 429-9292

Bilingual Vocational Oral Proficiency Test (BVOPT)

Author & Date
Melton Peninsula (1981)

Purpose
To assess the oral language proficiency of non-native English speakers--particularly proficiency needed to benefit from bilingual vocational training.

Description
There are four sections. The first asks the student twenty questions and looks for appropriate and understandable responses. The questions include several about the student, and then several about a series of five pictures. The second section asks the student to look at a series of pictures and "tell me everything you see in the pictures." The third section asks the student to repeat twenty sentences spoken by the administrator. The fourth section requires the student to move several objects on a table in accordance to a series of twenty imperative statements, such as, "Put the cup inside the box."

Administration
The instrument must be administered individually. The instructions to the students are simple and clear. The administrative procedures are moderately complex. The instructions for Section 1 are to be given in the student's native language, but are provided only in English. The instructions to the other sections are to be given in English, but the administrator is to clarify them, as needed, in the student's native language. There is no time limit. Most students finish within 30 minutes.

Alternate Forms
There are two approximately equivalent forms, Form A and Form B.

Reliability
Test-retest reliability is not reported in the manual. Internal consistency, measured by coefficient Alpha, has been mostly high (mostly .84 to .96)

Validity
The instrument reportedly was validated against the Nebraska Interview Schedule, but no validity data are reported in the manual. In the first and second sections of the instrument, important details in several pictures are obscure. In one question, the male

pronoun is used in reference to a child who is clearly wearing a dress. Several questions have no obviously correct answer.

Scoring & Interpretation

Scoring is moderately complex and takes about seven or eight minutes per student. The score on Section 1 is the number of questions "that received an appropriate and understandable response." Section 2 is scored holistically on a scale of 1 - 9, while listening to a tape recording of the student's response. Criteria for assigning the score are stated briefly, but no examples are given. The score on Section 3 is the number of statements that were "repeated perfectly or were repeated in a way that retained most of each statement's meaning." The score on Section 4 is the number of directions with which the student "does exactly what he/she is requested to do."

The raw score from each section must be changed to a "Converted Score" by use of conversion tables. The tables make the Section 1 scores twice as important as those of the other sections. No justification is given for this. A total score below 199 is considered to indicate low proficiency; a total score above 300 is considered high proficiency. No justification is given for those cutoffs.

Comments

This instrument was developed for adults, and is adult in content and tone. It was designed to focus on proficiency with linguistic structures that are most commonly used in work-place settings. These were determined to be: work-related directions about locations, work-related time relationships, instructions for work processes, work-related directions, work-related warnings and cautions, reasons for actions, evaluation statements about the quality of work performed, and statements of need.

Though this purpose is commendable, the manual for the instrument suggests that the authors were amateurs in respect to measurement. The instrument is repeatedly referred to as "criterion referenced," but the scoring procedure does not provide scores for specific skills. Such scores are the most important characteristic of criterion referenced instruments. The scoring procedures are judgmental, but inter-rater reliability was not studied, allegedly because "There was to be no effort made to establish norms for this Test." That is nonsense.

Availability

The instrument will be sold to anyone.

Price

The pictures to which the students are to respond cost $30.00. Sixty scoring forms cost $24.95. A copy of the manual, with both forms of the instrument, costs $12.95.

Source

Melton Book Company
161 Pittsburgh
Dallas, TX 75207
(800) 527-7830, or (214) 748-0564 in Texas

CASAS Adult Life Skills Language Tests

Author & Date
California Adult Student Assessment System (1984-87)

Purpose
To assess listening comprehension in common everyday life situations.

Description
There are 25 to 30 items, depending on which level of the instrument is used. All are multiple choice. The administrator gives directions or asks a question, and the student responds by selecting one of three alternative illustrations or sentences in the student booklet. At the lowest level, Level A, an example is: "Look at the pictures and listen. [The pictures are: a) a sheet of paper, b) a pencil, and c) a book.] What is the correct answer--A, B, or C? Give me a pencil. Is the answer A, B, or C?" At the highest level, Level C, an example is: "Look at the pictures and listen. [The pictures are of: a) a slice of pie, b) several cookies, and c) a slice of cake.] I'd like a piece of pie, please. Is the answer A, B, or C?"

At Levels A and B, when the response choices are sentences, they are orally presented by cassette tape. At level C, most of the items require reading at about the fifth grade level. There is just one score, the total number correct.

Administration
The instrument can be administered individually or to groups, but since the students respond to orally presented prompts, only one level and form can be administered in a group at one time. The instructions are simple and clear. All the oral prompts are played from a cassette tape. Because of that, the administration is paced and takes 28 to 44 minutes depending on which form of the instrument is being administered. Procedures for administration vary slightly from form to form.

Alternate Forms
There are three levels, A, B, and C, with the latter being the most advanced, and with two approximately equivalent forms at each level. At Level A there are forms L51 and L52; at Level B there are forms L53 and L54; at Level C there are forms L55 and L56. In addition, at Level B there are forms L63 and L64 that are for pre-vocational students, and at Level C there are forms L65 and L66 for pre-vocational students.

Reliability

No data on reliability were provided by the publisher, despite three requests for them. The instrument was constructed in the same manner as several other CASAS instruments. Those instruments have had high internal reliability, so this one probably does also.

Validity

No data showing correlations between scores on this instrument and other measures of similar life-skill competencies were provided by the publisher, despite three requests for them. It is likely that some learners who comprehend the spoken English directions and questions are unable to select the appropriate responses because of inadequate reading skills. This would be particularly true in ESL programs serving learners who are illiterate in their native language and those that focus exclusively on oral language instruction methods.

Scoring & Interpretation

Manual scoring is simple and quick. Norms data were not provided by the publisher, despite two requests for them. Computerized scoring is available from the publisher.

Comments

This instrument is used widely in California to evaluate outcomes of English as a Second Language programs. It was specifically developed for adults. A commendable array of life-skills materials are included, and most people will find it useful in daily living to master the aural comprehension that is measured by the instrument.

This is one of the very few instruments for measuring oral English skills that does not have to be administered to one learner at a time. But because it is was designed for group administration, it only assesses the comprehension of oral English, not also the speaking of English. Some learners have comprehension skills that are substantially above their speaking skills.

There are only three response choices in the student booklets, but the answer sheets that are used if computerized scoring is to be done by the publisher have four response choices. It seems inevitable that students will err occasional and mark the "d" column when they intended to mark the "c" column.

Availability

This instrument is available to educational organizations, but they must go through training provided by CASAS before using it.

Price

Twenty-five student booklets of one form cost $30.00. No price is reported for the answer sheets. The brief manual is distributed with no charge. Write or call for information on the cost of the training that is required before using this instrument.

Source

CASAS
2725 Congress Street, #1-M
San Diego, CA 92110
(619) 298-4681

English as a Second Language Oral Assessment (ESLOA)

Author & Date

Joyce Jenkins Coy and others (1978-80)

Purpose

To efficiently measure the ability of non-native English speakers to speak and understand English.

Description

The instrument is divided into four progressively more difficult levels. The student is judged as being at level 1, 2, 3, or 4, depending on how many levels he or she successfully completes. There is a total of 41 items. At the first level, the student is shown drawings with three objects and asked questions like: "Where is the box?" or "Which girl is walking?" The student may respond orally or by pointing. At the second level, the student is asked to answer simple questions and name illustrated objects. At the third level, the student is shown drawings and asked questions such as: "What is he doing?" and "Where is she going?" The student must respond orally, and is encouraged to use complete sentences. The student is also orally given several sentences and asked to modify them in a specified manner, such as from statements to questions. At the fourth level, the student is orally given sentences and asked to change them to different tenses, shown pictures and asked what is happening in them, and told of specific circumstances and asked what he or she would do in them. There also is an optional section that provides a simple means for judging spoken English in response to personal questions such as: "What television shows do you like? Why?"

Administration

The instrument must be administered individually. Administration is simple. It is terminated when a student misses more than a specified number of items in any of the four sections. There is no time limit; administration of all four levels will seldom take more than twenty minutes.

Alternate Forms

There is only one form.

Reliability

The publisher does not have reliability data.

116

Validity

The publisher does not have validity data. Inexplicably, there are a substantial number of items that require naming parts of the human body and articles of clothing, but few items that deal with food, housing, work, and transportation.

Scoring & Interpretation

Manual scoring is simple and quick. The score for each level of the instrument is the number of correctly answered items in that level. The manual does not report any norm data.

Comments

This instrument was specifically designed for adults, but few of the items deal with the activities that occupy most adults' time--working, meal preparation, house keeping, and child raising. The instrument focuses on beginning and intermediate English. People scoring at the highest level, Level 4, could easily have difficulty understanding and participating in conversational English. No reading is required of the student.

Availability

This instrument is available to anyone.

Price

The manual with the instrument pictures costs $6.00. Fifty answer sheets cost $2.00.

Source

Literacy Volunteers of America
5795 Widewaters Parkway
Syracuse, NY 13214
(315) 445-8000

The John Test / The Fred Test

Author & Date

Language Innovations, Inc. (1975-83)

Purpose

To assess oral proficiency for placement in non-academic ESL programs.

Description

The student is initially asked a few personal questions. If able to respond, he or she is given Parts 1-3. In Part 1, labeled "Comprehension Questions," The student is shown seven drawings depicting events in the daily life of John or Fred, and asked two to four questions about each picture. The questions are like "What is on the ... ?" and "Is he ...? How do you know?" In Part 2, labeled "Connected Discourse," the student is told, "Now I want you to tell me the story of John's/Fred's day YESTERDAY. For example, yesterday he got up, then ...." In Part 3, labeled "Asking Questions," the student is told "I want you to ask me some questions about John/Fred. I'll tell you what questions to ask. For example, ask me how old he is."

Administration

This instrument must be administered individually. Administration is moderately complex. Some of the instructions for the students are in the manual rather than on the scoring sheet that has the questions to be read to the students. In Part 1, the questions are to be read with "normal speed and intonation."

The instructions to the students are simple, but incomplete and sometimes unclear. In Part 1, the student is not told that he or she may ask the administrator to repeat any question, yet the administrator is to do so only if the student makes the request. In Part 2, the student is told to tell a story about John or Fred's "day yesterday." It is not clear whether the drawings are supposed to be of yesterday, and thus the student is to summarize the events shown, or whether the student is to describe another imagined day in the life of John or Fred. In Part 3, the instructions are "I want you to ask me some questions... I'll tell you what questions to ask...." This requires comprehension of a convoluted and seldom used English construction.

The administration is paced. It usually takes 10 - 15 minutes.

Alternate Forms

There is only one level of the instrument. There are two roughly equivalent forms called "The John Test" and "The Fred Test."

Reliability

Test-retest reliability, using alternate forms of the instrument, has been high (.95). Inter-rater reliability, which is important in judgmental scoring, is not reported.

Validity

No validity data are provided in the brief manual.

Scoring & Interpretation

Scoring is moderately complex because it is judgmental and most of it is done as the instrument is being administered. The story the student tells in Part 2 is to be judged in respect to fluency, structure, pronunciation, and vocabulary. The manual provides some guidelines on how to assess each. Very limited norm data are provided for an unspecified group of 96 students.

Comments

The instrument is adult in content and tone. One-forth of the questions in Part 1 are about matters that are not clear from the illustrations. For instance, accompanying a drawing showing only the very front of a bus, there is the question, "Is there a man with a ... on the bus?" None of the three men shown has the specified feature, but there could be other people, not shown, who do have the feature. Some other questions are tricky, because they misidentify characteristics in the drawings. For instance, one asks why a specific person is in a specified posture, but the person is actually in another posture.

Part 1 is labeled "Comprehension Questions," but full credit is possible only, "If [each response] is what a native speaker of English would say...." Any request that a question be restated results in deduction of half-credit for the question, and the student is not forewarned of this.

There is so much ambiguity in the instructions and prompts, that native English speaking Ph.D.s probably will not average more than 93 percent of the maximum score. ESL students could easily score less than they are able by: 1) not answering when the correct answer is unclear, 2) asking that the question be repeated when the answer is unclear (and losing half-credit), or 3) becoming rattled because they think the confusion is due to their lack of English skills.

A 1987 review (in Reviews of English Language Proficiency Tests, pg. 47) says this instrument has been used successfully to place students in ESL classes, but that many users drop Part 3 or otherwise adapt the instrument. It also says the validity of the instrument as a general measure of oral proficiency is limited because the full range of survival competencies are not included.

Availability

The instrument is available to everyone.

Price

One copy of the John test and the John/Fred manual will be provided free. Permission is granted to duplicate these materials for non-commercial purposes.. Check with the source about arrangements for the Fred test.

Source

Riverside Adult Learning Center
490 Riverside Drive
New York, NY 10027
(212) 222-5900 ext. 115

Language Assessment Scales-Oral (LAS-O)

Author & Date
Edward De Avila & Sharon Duncan (1981-87)

Purpose
To measure oral proficiency in both English and Spanish.

Description
Only the English proficiency instrument is reviewed here. There are five sections. The section on minimal pairs has 24 or 30 items that measure auditory discrimination. Two words, like "read/lead" and "beet/bet" are orally presented and the student is to indicate if they "sound the same or different." The section on vocabulary presents 20 pictures and the student is to "say what they are." The section on phonemes has 36 items, each consisting of a specific phoneme embedded once in a orally presented word and twice in a sentence, such as "four" and "The wolf was laughing;" The student is to repeat the word and the sentence. The section on sentence comprehension orally presents 10 sentences of various syntactic structures and the student is to indicate which of three drawings "best goes with what you hear." The section on oral production shows the student four related pictures, orally presents a short story about them, and asks the student to listen carefully and afterwards "retell it in your own words."

Administration
The instrument must be administered individually. Administration is moderately complex. Instructions are first given by the administrator to the student in "whatever language, mixture of languages, or dialects are necessary for the student to understand." An audio tape presents the oral stimuli to which the student responds. In two of the sections, the administrator is to rewind and replay any stimulus with which the student is having difficulty. For the oral production section, the administrator is to write down everything the student says, and score it later. In the other four sections, scoring is to be done simultaneously with administration. The administration is not timed. Most students finish within 20 minutes.

Alternate Forms
There are two levels. Level I is for students in grades K-5, and Level II is for students in grades 6-12. At each level there are separate instruments for measuring oral Spanish

121

proficiency and oral English proficiency, and there are two approximately equivalent forms of the latter.

Reliability

Test-retest reliability is not reported in the Technical Supplements. KR-20 has been moderate to high for the section scores (.67 to .97). Inter-rater reliability for scoring of the oral production section, using three highly trained judges, has been high (.79 to .96).

Validity

The average scores of monolingual English speakers have been substantially higher than those of language minority students on every section in Level I except that for phonemes, but in Level II the differences have been small. Correlations between the newer Forms B and the older Forms A have been moderate to high (.59 to .96).

Scoring & Interpretation

Scoring is complex. For the vocabulary section, synonyms and near synonyms are acceptable, but if the term is much less specific (such as "fruit" for an apple) the student is to be asked "What kind of ...?" The phoneme items are judged correct if the student is able to repeat the phonemes embedded in the item "in such a fashion that he/she would not be misunderstood or ridiculed." The oral production section is to be judged holistically on a scale of 0-5. A "2" represents mostly very simple sentences or fragments, and little story line. A "5" represents sentences that are complete, coherent, and grammatically correct for the student's "developmental age." Extensive examples of what would be a 1, 2, 3, 4, and 5 for each age group are provided, but considerable training and practice is probably needed for reliable scoring. Conventional norm data are not provided in the Technical Supplements, despite a subtitle that indicates these publications include norms.

Comments

This instrument was developed for elementary and secondary students. The content and tone of Level I is definitely juvenile, but Level II is generally adult.

A 1987 review (in Reviews of English Language Proficiency Tests, pg. 51) says this is an acceptable instrument, but that the evidence of validity is not strong.

Availability

The instrument will be sold to teachers "in institutions or agencies with signed approval on the CTB order form of his or her administrator."

Price

The picture cue books cost $11.60 for any one level and form. Fifty answer sheets for any one level and form cost $31.25. A specimen set for any one level, including two of three manuals, costs $25.00. The three manuals (and all three are needed) cost $6.00, $14.00, and $21.50.

Source

CTB/McGraw-Hill
2500 Garden Road
Monterey, CA 93940
(800) 538-9547, or (408) 649-8400 from outside the continental United

Language Facility Test
(LFT)

Author & Date
John Diley (1965-80)

Purpose
To measure oral language facility in English or Spanish.

Description
Students are shown three pictures, one at a time, and asked to tell a story about each. The instructions are given verbally; no reading is required of the student. The pictures are of everyday life; most include children and many include at least one adult. Many are photographs, but a few are drawings.

Administration
The instrument is administered individually. It is not timed, but seldom takes more than 10 minutes. The procedures are simple. The instructions are given orally.

Alternate Forms
Twelve pictures are provided in the kit and a sample of three is generally used with each student. The scores from each picture correlate moderately (about .7). Complete instructions are given for administering the instrument in Spanish.

Reliability
Test-retest reliabilities have ranged from moderately low to high (.46 to .90).

Validity
Correlations with several standard language instruments (including the Metropolitan Readiness Test, Stanford Achievement Test, and Peabody Picture Vocabulary Test) were all low (less than .37) for first and second graders. The correlation with teachers' ratings of students' oral language performance was very low (.05).

This instrument seems aimed more at measuring story telling than oral language usage. The former obviously involves language usage, but it involves more than that. The scoring system requires mention of "past or future action or intentions" and use of "imagination and creativity" for the higher scores. Because of incomplete instructions, the instrument probably is not even a valid measure of story telling. The instructions do not state that the story should go beyond a straight forward description. Indeed, the prompts given following an "incomplete" story can be misleading. They are, "Tell me what you see in the picture" and "What are they doing in the picture." A literal interpretation of those instructions foredooms the student to a mediocre score.

Scoring & Interpretation

There are two ways to score the responses. One is holistically on a scale from zero to nine. Zero is for no response, garbled speech, or only pointing at the picture; six is for a detailed description of what is happening, but nothing about past or future action or intentions; and nine is for a well-organized story with imagination and creativity. Detailed guidelines for the scoring and plentiful examples are given. Though the scoring involves judgment, there is evidence that people can do it very similarly after careful training. Norm data for this form of scoring are given for about 2,500 students, age 3 to 20. The second form of scoring tallies 24 types of deviations from standard English usage. There is little explanation of this scoring in the manual and no norms for the scores are provided.

Comments

This instrument was designed for children age 3 to 15, and has primarily been used with them. The materials and instructions would probably not seem condescending to most adults, but they also would not be considered of high interest to them.

A 1985 review (The Ninth Mental Measurements Yearbook, #585) concluded this instrument has not been verified as a valid measure of language competence or proficiency and it should not be used for that purpose.

Availability

The instrument is sold to anyone.

Price

A complete kit with twelve pictures, an administrator's manual, the Spanish administration instructions, and selected references costs $22.50. One hundred answer sheets cost $12.00.

Source

The Allington Corporation
P.O. Box 125
Remington, VA 22734
(703) 825-5722

Listening Comprehension Test (LCT)

Author & Date

John Upshur and others 1972-1986

Purpose

To assess non-native speakers' understanding of spoken English, especially for persons who wish to pursue academic work at colleges and universities where English is the medium of instruction.

Description

The students listen to a tape recording that presents 45 short statements and questions. After each statement or question there is a pause and the student is to look at his or her booklet and select the appropriate response from three alternatives. When a question has been asked, the correct response is an acceptable answer. An example is: "When are you going? a) I am b) Tomorrow c) At home." When a statement has been made, the correct response is a second statement that shows understanding of the initial one. An example is: "The camera on the desk is expensive. a) The camera is expensive. b) The desk is expensive. c) The camera and the desk are expensive." Answers are recorded on a separate answer sheet. A single score of aural comprehension is computed.

Administration

The instrument can be administered individually or to a group. It is timed, with twelve second pauses after each question or statement, and takes a total of fifteen minutes. The instructions are simple, but some students may be confused by the fact that the orally presented sentences include statements as well as questions.

Alternate Forms

There are three equivalent forms, Forms 4, 5, and 6.

Reliability

Test-retest reliability is not reported in the manual even though the needed data were collected. KR-21 reliability has been high (.80).

Validity

Scores on this instrument correlate moderately with those on it's predecessor, the Michigan Test of Aural Comprehension, and with the Michigan Test of English

Language Proficiency (.76 and .65, respectively). The former, however, has not been well validated and the latter measures different skills, so these correlations don't provide good evidence of the instrument's validity.

Few of the orally presented statements and questions to which the student responds are longer than twelve words in length. It is reasonable to wonder whether all students who score well with such items would also score well with longer ones.

Scoring & Interpretation

Manual scoring is simple and quick. Norm data are based on 1486 non-native English speaking applicants to U.S. colleges and universities. The data are also reported for each of several native languages, but little other information is given about the applicants.

Comments

This instrument was developed for adults and is appropriate for them in both content and tone. Most of the items are about everyday events that are common to all people's lives. The instrument was developed as a successor to the Michigan Test of Aural Comprehension, which is longer, but otherwise very similar . It assesses intermediate and advanced proficiency. Though used to assess understanding of spoken English, it requires reading to select the appropriate response from the student booklet. Most of the response options are three to five word sentences. The reading level is about at the 4th grade level. Given that the instrument is intended primarily for applicants to colleges, this is not unreasonable. A 1987 review of this instrument's predecessor (in Reviews of English Language Proficiency Tests, pg. 60) indicates that it appears to mainly measure grammar skills.

Availability

The instrument will be sold to bona fide educational institutions and researchers.

Price

Twenty reusable student booklets cost $5.00. One hundred answer sheets cost $5.00. The cassette costs $12.00. The manual costs $2.50. A specimen set, including a copy of the manual, costs $8.00.

Source

ELI Test Publications
English Language Institute
The University of Michigan
Ann Arbor, MI 48109-1057
(313) 747-0456

Michigan Test Of Aural Comprehension (MTAC)

Author & Date

John Upshur and others (1969-1972)

Purpose

To measure the ability of non-native speakers of English to understand orally presented English, particularly the ability of persons wishing to enroll in colleges and universities where instruction is provided in English.

Description

The student is read 90 statements and questions by the examiner, or hears them when a tape recording is played. After each statement or question there is a pause and the student is to look at his or her booklet and select the appropriate response from three alternatives. When a question has been asked, the correct response is an acceptable answer. When a statement has been made, the correct response is a second statement that shows understanding of the initial one. An example item is: "Are you busy? a) Yes, I am; b) Yes, you are; c) Yes, he is." Another example is: "I've just begun. a) I am almost finished; b) I just finished; c) I just started." Answers are recorded on a separate answer sheet. A single score of aural comprehension is computed.

Administration

The instrument can be administered individually or to a group. It is timed, with fifteen second pauses after each statement or question. Administration takes about 23 minutes. The instructions are neither simple nor complex. Some students may be confused by the fact that the orally presented sentences include statements as well as questions.

Alternate Forms

There are several secured forms that are restricted to use in admissions screening at colleges and universities. There are other forms that are unsecured.

Reliability

No reliability data are reported in the manual.

Validity

The manual for this instrument does not report validity data. The manual for another instrument, the Michigan Test of English Language Proficiency (reviewed separately in this handbook) indicates that scores on this instrument have correlated moderately to highly (.67 to .85) with the scores on that one. Since the two instruments are supposed to measure different language skills, that result does not substantiate the validity of this instrument.

Few of the orally presented statements and questions to which the student responds are longer than twelve words in length. It is reasonable to wonder whether all students who score well with such items would also score well with longer ones.

Scoring & Interpretation

Manual scoring is simple and quick. Norm data, based on 1180 persons, are reported in the manual for the Michigan Test of English Language Proficiency. The data are reported for each of several native languages, but little other information is given about these persons.

Comments

This instrument was designed to assess intermediate and advanced proficiency. Though it is used to assess understanding of spoken English, it requires reading to select the appropriate response from the student booklet. Most of the response options are three to five word sentences. The reading level is about at the 4th grade level. Given that the instrument is intended primarily for college applicants, this is not unreasonable. Most of the items are about everyday events that are common to all people's lives. A 1987 review (in Reviews of English Language Proficiency Tests, pg. 60) indicates that this instrument appears to mainly measure grammar skills.

Availability

The unsecured forms of the instrument are available to ESL instructors.

Price

Twenty reusable student booklets cost $8.50. One hundred answer sheets cost $5.00. The manual costs $2.50. Cassette tapes cost $18.00. A specimen set, including a copy of the manual, costs $8.00.

Source

ELI Test Publications
English Language Institute
The University of Michigan
Ann Arbor, MI 48109-1057
(313) 747-0456

Oral English/Spanish Proficiency Placement Tests

Author & Date
Steve Moreno (1974-76)

Purpose
To assess the English or Spanish listening and speaking proficiency of bilingual and native Spanish speaking persons.

Description
The student is shown eight drawings, each depicting two children, Juan and Maria, and several objects. For each drawing the student is asked questions or told to make statements such as: "What does Maria have?" "Where do you sleep at home?" and "Ask me, 'May I eat the cookies?'" The student responds orally. There are 151 items. There is only one score, the total number of correct responses.

Administration
The instrument must be administered individually. It generally does not take more than 15 minutes. The instructions are simple and clear. The administration is stopped whenever a student misses any three of four consecutive items.

Alternate Forms
There is an English and a Spanish form of the instrument. The exercises are identical, except that the questions asked by the administrator and the responses to be given by the student are to be in English or Spanish.

Reliability
Test-retest reliability is high (.85 to .94).

Validity
The scores correlate moderately highly (.72 to .85) with teacher judgments.

Scoring & Interpretation
Manual scoring is moderately complex, but takes only a minute or two. Each oral response of the student is judged by the administrator, but only a specified part of each response is judged, and the rest is to be ignored. Examples of acceptable responses are given, but other equally proficient responses are possible. Norms are reported in the manual, but only for an unspecified number of inner city children in an unspecified city.

Comments

This instrument was designed for placement of children in the publisher's curriculum materials. The pictures and the questions are distinctly juvenile in content. Some adults would probably find them uninteresting or condescending. The instrument measures beginning listening and speaking skills. The highest score is said to be equivalent to the skill of the average monolingual English speaking child who is completing kindergarten.

A 1985 review (in The Ninth Mental Measurements Yearbook #902) points out several shortcomings of the instrument and the guidelines for interpreting the scores. It concludes, however, that the instrument may be useful as a gross measure of language proficiency.

Availability

The instrument is available to anyone.

Price

The manual, with the pictures, costs $13.95. The answer sheets cost $0.30 apiece.

Source

Moreno Educational Company
7050 Belle Glade Lane
San Diego, CA 92119
(619) 461-0565

Secondary Level English Proficiency Test (SLEP)

Author & Date
Educational Testing Service (1980-1987)

Purpose
To assess the understanding of spoken and written English of non-native English speaking students who are entering grades seven through twelve.

Description
The section assessing listening skills has four types of exercises, all asking the student to respond to statements on an audio tape. The first type requires that the student match one of four spoken statements with a picture. The second type requires matching a spoken statement with one of four alternative statements printed in the student booklet. The third type presents a map with four cars marked a, b, c, and d on it. Brief conversations of the occupants of the cars are presented orally, and the student responds by indicating in which car the conversation took place. The forth type presents a brief spoken conversation and asks the student to answer questions about it by selecting one of four printed statements.

The section assessing reading also has four types of exercises. There are 75 items in each of the two sections. Scores are computed for listening comprehension, reading comprehension, and total.

Administration
The instrument can be administered individually or to a group. Administration of the instrument and instructions for the students are simple and clear. There is a time limit of forty-five minutes for each section.

Alternate Forms
There are two forms, 1 and 2.

Reliability
Test-retest reliability is not reported. KR-20 has been high (.94 to .96).

Validity
There is a correlation (the magnitude is not specified) between both scores on this instrument and the score on the Language Assessment Scales II, which judges actual

student speaking. The two scores also correlated moderately highly (.74 and .80) with the comparable scores on the Test of English as a Foreign Language. The latter instrument is more difficult, as it should be, since it is designed for foreign applicants to U.S. and Canadian colleges. In the study that established the norms, the mean scores of students in full-time bilingual education programs were the lowest, followed by those in part-time bilingual programs, full-time ESL, part-time ESL, and regular programs -- just as one would expect from a valid measure of language.

Scoring & Interpretation

Manual scoring is simple and moderately quick. Norm data from 1,239 non-native English speakers enrolled in 68 U.S. public high schools in 1980-81 are presented in the manual. The scores are reported by several characteristics of the students.

Comments

This instrument was developed for high school students. The material does not appear to be condescending to adults, but most of it has a middle class orientation. Items in the listening comprehension section require reading at about the 4th grade level.

A 1985 review (in the Ninth Mental Measurements Yearbook, #1090) said the closest competitor of this instrument appears to be A Comprehensive English Language Test for Speakers of English as a Second Language. A 1987 review (in Reviews of English Language Proficiency Tests, pg. 68) recommended the use of this instrument for assessing listening and reading skills, but noted it does not assess speaking skills.

It appears to this reviewer that a moderate portion of students will have some trouble understanding the instructions. The instrument uses a variety of items, and several of them are not common. A brochure describing the instrument provides several examples of each type of item. Instructors preparing students to take this instrument should consider using the brochure to familiarize students with the exercises.

Availability

The instrument is available to accredited secondary educational institutions. Under appropriate circumstances the materials will also be sold to others engaged in legitimate evaluation activities.

Price

A complete kit with 20 reusable student booklets, 100 answer sheets, the cassette tape, the manual, and two scoring keys costs $100.00. A specimen set, including a copy of the manual, costs $15.00.

Source

Educational Testing Service
Rosedale Road
Princeton, NJ 08541
(609) 771-7244

The Second Language Oral Test of English (SLOTE)

Author & Date
Ann K. Fathman (1983)

Purpose
To assess the ability of non-native English speakers to produce standard English grammatical structures.

Description
The instrument has sixty items. There are three items to measure each of 20 grammatical structures, such as declaratives, present participles, superlatives, present tense third person irregular, prepositions, past participles--regular, negatives, subject pronouns, possessive pronouns, plurals--irregular, and wh- questions. All exercises are in response to pictures. One practice item shows a picture of a woman holding a cat and another woman holding books. The administrator points to the first woman and says, "Here the mother has the cat." Then he or she points to the second woman and says, "Here the mother has _____." The student is to say, "some books." Another picture shows one large and two smaller balls. The administrator points to the large one and says, "This ball is big." Then he points to the second one and says, "But this ball is _____." The student is to say "little."

Administration
The SLOTE is normally administered individually. The instructions for the student are simple, but not clear. The student is only told, "Now we will look at some pictures of a family and talk about them.... I will describe the first and you will continue when I look at you." The manual says, "If the procedure is not understood after 2 attempts, have the student repeat the entire description with you, then try again." The student is not directed to use good English and is not told the correct answers to the five practice items if he or she gets them wrong. The administration is done orally, and the student is given a maximum of 20 seconds to respond to each item. Usually the administration is completed within 20 minutes.

Alternate Forms
There is just one form.

Reliability

Test-retest reliability, after one week, has been quite high (.97 to .98). KR-20 has also been high (.95). Scoring involves some judgment, but inter-rater reliability is not reported. There is indirect evidence that it can be high, but that is based on just two raters, and there is no indication of their prior expertise in English grammar, nor of the nature and duration of training they received in scoring this instrument.

Validity

Sub-scores on the SLOTE for six grammatical structures have had low to high correlations (.46 to .80) with expert linguists' ratings of the students use of these structures in free speech. The overall SLOTE score has correlated moderately (.68) with the linguists' ratings of the students' grammatical correctness, and highly (.81) with instructors' ratings of the students' grammatical proficiency. The instrument also has exhibited high correlations (mostly in the .80s) with other oral language instruments.

Scoring & Interpretation

Scoring is somewhat judgmental. The common correct variants and the common incorrect variants are given in the manual. The administrator is urged to score items as the student responds to them. Alternatively, the manual suggests tape recording the responses and scoring them after. That is probably advisable for the non-linguist, at least until he or she has considerable experience with the scoring, but it will almost double the amount of time needed to administer and score the instrument. There are no norm data in the manual.

Comments

The SLOTE was designed for beginning and intermediate level English speakers. The content and tone are generally juvenile. Most of the pictures are of children. The responses required of the students are generally simple descriptions of the pictures.

A strength of this instrument is that it measures skill with 20 grammatical structures, each with three items presented one after the other. That makes it easy to identify the structures that the student has not mastered. But the SLOTE does not measure pronunciation or fluency.

A 1987 review (in Reviews of English Language Proficiency Tests, pg. 67) recommended the instrument for use with beginning and intermediate students. It noted, however, that the structures are not in the order normally mastered, so administration with beginning students cannot be terminated when they miss several consecutive items.

Availability

This instrument will be sold to anyone.

Price

The manual, which includes all the materials needed to administer the instrument, costs $16.95. Scoring sheets are not available from the publisher, but can easily be prepared locally.

Source

Alemany Press
2501 Industrial Parkway West
Hayward, CA 94545
(800) 227-2375, or (415) 887-7070 in California

Test of English as a Foreign Language (TOEFL)

Author & Date
Educational Testing Service (1963-87)

Purpose
To assess the English proficiency of non-native English speakers, especially those applying to study in English speaking colleges and universities.

Description
The instrument has three sections, each with its own score. The section on listening comprehension has three parts. One presents a spoken sentence, and the student is to select which of four written sentences is closest in meaning. The second presents a short spoken conversation followed by a spoken question about the conversation, and the student is to select which of four written responses is the correct answer. The third part presents several spoken sentences followed by a spoken question about them, and the student is to select which of four written responses is the correct answer. The section on structure and written expression presents a written sentence with a missing word, and the student must select, from four written alternatives, the word that best completes the sentence. It also presents a written sentence with four underlined words, and the student is to indicate which word needs to be changed to comply with the rules of proper English. The section on vocabulary and reading comprehension presents a sentence with one underlined word, and the student is to select, from four others, a replacement that best keeps the meaning of the original sentence. It also presents a short passage and the student is to answer multiple choice questions about it. Optionally, a Test of Written English is also administered.

Administration
The instrument is administered under the direct supervision of the publisher, several times a year, at about 100 centers in the United States and about 1,000 internationally. Forms of the instrument that are recently retired from use at these centers are available for administration by colleges and other agencies. There are time limits of 35, 25, and 45 minutes for the three sections. At least eighty percent of the students usually complete all items in each of the three sections.

Alternate Forms
New forms are developed frequently and standardized against the prior forms.

Reliability

Test-retest reliability is not reported. Internal consistency has been high (.86 to .90) for the section scores and even higher (.95) for the total score. Inter-scorer reliability for the written essay has been moderately high (.73 to .75).

Validity

Scores on the TOEFL have correlated highly with several other comprehensive measures of English language proficiency, including one used at U.C. Berkeley in 1965 (.87), The Michigan Test of English Language Proficiency (.89), an instrument developed by the American Language Institute(.79), and teacher ratings (.76 to .87).

Scoring & Interpretation

Scoring is done only by the publisher. It takes four to twelve weeks for the results to be returned. The essay is scored holistically on a six-point scale by two trained English specialists. If their scores are within one point, they are averaged. If not, the score is adjudicated by the chief reader. Norm data are based on 714,000 persons who took the TOEFL in 1984-1986. Norms are reported separately for undergraduate applicants, graduate applicants, other students, and applicants for professional licensure. Most U.S. and Canadian colleges require a score of at least 500 for admission.

Comments

This is the most widely used measure of ESL in the world. In 1985 over 450,000 people took it. More than 3,000 institutions, mostly U.S. colleges and universities, require TOEFL scores when considering foreign student applicants.

The instrument measures a wide range of language skills. Required reading is at about the sixth grade level for the sections on listening and written expression, and at about the ninth grade level for the section on vocabulary and reading. A recent review (in Reviews of English Language Proficiency Tests, page 79) concluded that TOEFL is "the best of its breed."

Availability

Forms no longer used at the publisher's test centers are available to "colleges, universities, and agencies" to administer to their own students, but the publisher still does the scoring.

Price

Use of retired forms of the instrument at a local site is $10.00 per person, including computerized scoring by the publisher. To take the instrument at an authorized test center costs $27.00 to $35.00. The TOEFL Sample Test, complete with a phonograph record to simulate the standard administration procedures, costs $3.00.

Source

Educational Testing Service
TOEFL Programs and Services
CN 6151
Princeton, NJ 08541-6151
(609) 882-6601

Affective
Outcomes

Introduction

The instruments reviewed in this section measure self-esteem or self-determination. Several are comprehensive personality batteries, also measuring other characteristics.

Self-esteem involves a sense of worth, competency, efficacy, respect, acceptance, and well-being. It can be in reference to physical, intellectual, emotional, moral-ethical, and social self. It also can be in reference to family, school, work, community, and other settings. Self-esteem is usually assessed in terms of how one perceives herself (self-perception), but sometimes it is also assessed in terms of how one thinks others perceive her (reflected self-esteem) or in terms of how one wants to be (ideal self).

Self-determination includes: self-direction, independence, initiative, planning, confidence, perseverance, efficacy, and responsibility. It is usually assessed by self perceptions, but it can be assessed by other persons' perceptions or by behavior inventories.

Though high self-esteem and self-determination are positive traits, extremely high scores often indicate delusions of grandeur, denial of shortcomings, or faking socially desirable responses. A few of the instruments include a "lie scale" to detect these; others just warn that very high scores may indicate serious misrepresentations.

Some people enjoy responding to these instruments. They find it similar to talking about one's self. Other people are bothered about the personal nature of the questions and their obscure purposes. This reviewer has considerable experience administering the Culture-Free Self-Esteem Inventory to adult literacy students. His review of that instrument reports some disturbing reactions by students to the instrument, as well as some very positive ones. It is not clear whether these reactions would occur when using the other self-esteem instruments. Many could be criticized by students for similar reasons, but most are lacking lie-scale items, and these items of the Culture-Free were considered the most offensive.

Many of the instruments present written self-description statements and ask the students to indicate whether each statement is "usually true" for them or "usually not true." The required reading ranges from Grade 4 - 8. Such instruments can easily be administered orally to groups, if the students can read numbers and the words "true" and "false." This modification should not affect the validity of the responses. Some of the instruments, however, are ill-suited for oral administration because they use sophisticated vocabulary, more complex response choices, or several hundred items.

Instruments that Measure Affective Characteristics

Instrument	Page	Reading requirements
Adult Personality Inventory (API)	147	At least Grade 5 reading
Bloom Sentence Completion Survey (BSCS)	149	No reading
California Psychological Inventory (CPI)	151	At least Grade 6 reading
Coopersmith Self-Esteem Inventory (SEI)	154	At least Grade 4 reading*
Culture-Free Self Esteem Inventories	156	At least Grade 5 reading*
The Facial Interpersonal Perception Inventory (FIPI)	159	No reading
Gordon Personal Profile-Inventory (GPP-I)	161	At least Grade 7 reading
Interpersonal Style Inventory (ISI)	164	At least Grade 7 reading
Jackson Personality Inventory (JPI)	166	At least Grade 7 reading
The Schutz Measures--Element S: Self-Concept	168	At least Grade 7 reading
Self-Concept Evaluation of Location Form (SELF)	170	At least Grade 5 reading*
Self-Description Inventory	172	At least Grade 8 reading
Self-Directed Learning Readiness Scale (SDLRS)	174	At least Grade 4 reading*
Self-Esteem Questionnaire (SEQ-3)	176	At least Grade 5 reading*
Self-Observation Scales (SOS)	178	At least Grade 6 reading*
Self-Perception Inventory (SPI)	180	At least Grade 8 reading
Tennessee Self-Concept Scale (TSCS)	182	At least Grade 6 reading*
Wahler Self-Description Inventory (WSDI)	184	At least Grade 6 reading*

* These instruments can easily be administered orally so that students with a reading skills at only Grade 1 can respond. See text for more details.

Adult Personality Inventory (API)

Author & Date
Samuel E. Krug (1982-86)

Purpose
To assess individual differences in personality, interpersonal style, and career and life-style preferences.

Description
Most of the 324 items are brief self-descriptions, to which the student is to respond "generally true," "uncertain," or "generally false." There are statements like: "I usually make good decisions," and, "I feel uncomfortable in groups of people." A total of thirty items require selecting similar words, doing mathematical computations, and detecting analogies. The instrument yields the following seven scores for personality characteristics: extroverted, adjusted, tough-minded, independent, disciplined, creative, and enterprising. It yields the following eight scores for interpersonal style: caring, adapting, withdrawn, submissive, hostile, rebellious, sociable, and assertive. And it yields the following six scores for career and life-style preferences: practical, scientific, aesthetic, social, competitive, and structured.

Administration
The instrument can be administered individually or to a group. Administration is simple, but the instructions to the student might cause some confusion. General instructions are followed by a warning that "Several parts have separate instructions...." Part 1 has no instructions, and Parts 2, 3, and 4 are preceded by brief instructions that differ some from the general instructions. Students are permitted to ask questions and any confusions probably can be cleared up quickly. The instrument is not timed. The publisher claims that most students will finish it within an hour, but low-level readers will probably need more time because of the large number of items.

Alternate Forms
There is just one form.

Reliability
The manual was not reviewed.

Validity

The manual was not reviewed.

Scoring & Interpretation

The instrument cannot be manually scored because it requires complex formulas (multiple regression equations) and the publisher's computerized scoring costs a minimum of $7.90 per student. Norm data are available.

Comments

A specimen set was not ordered and reviewed. Computerized scoring by the publisher is required and costly, making this instrument prohibitively expensive for most adult literacy programs.

The instrument was developed for adults. It requires about a 5th grade level of reading. Low-level readers may find it frustrating to be confronted with such a large number of items.

A 1985 review (in The Ninth Mental Measurements Yearbook, #54) concluded that API scores are relevant for counseling and personnel purposes.

Availability

A note at the bottom of the order form states that this instrument "is sold only to appropriately qualified individuals." No explanation of that statement is given and no qualifications have to be reported on the form.

Price

Ten reusable student booklets cost $12.80. Twenty-five answer sheets cost $7.50. The manual costs $12.75. A specimen kit, including the manual and prepaid processing of one answer sheet, costs $23.50. Computerized scoring costs $16.00 per person when 1-4 answer sheets are submitted at one time. The cost drops to $10.90 in quantities of 5-24 and to $7.90 in quantities of 100 or more. The scoring includes an eight-page detailed report on each person's scores.

Source

Institute for Personality and Ability Testing
P.O. Box 188
Champaign, IL 61820-0188
(800) 225-4728, or (217) 352-4739 within Illinois

Bloom Sentence Completion Survey (BSCS)

Author & Date
Wallace Bloom (1974)

Purpose
To reveal attitudes toward self, others, work, and accomplishment.

Description
There are forty phrases that begin a sentence and the student is to respond to each, completing the sentence. The phrases are like: " Most employers _____," "People usually think I _____," and "My mind is _____" There are eight scores--for attitudes toward people, physical self, family, psychological self, self-directedness, work, accomplishment, and irritants.

Administration
The instrument is administered individually and usually takes less than 25 minutes. Several of the items have to be pre-edited to take into account the student's sex and marital status. The instructions are simple, but might be interpreted differently by different students. They tell the student to "finish it [the sentence] with the first thing that comes to your mind, regardless of whether it is true or untrue, correct or silly." For items that yield responses that are "ambiguous... [or] only descriptive, objective, or evasive" an "inquiry" is to be made at the end, in hopes of revealing an attitude. But the manual does not suggest ways of making that inquiry.

Alternate Forms
There is just one form.

Reliability
Test-retest and internal reliability are not reported in the manual. Since each score is based on just five items, the reliability of the scores is probably not high.

Validity
The manual reports considerable validity data, but little of it is convincing. Scores on this instrument have correlated some (the magnitude is not reported) with whether Air Force recruits pass a mental health screening soon after entering the service. Correlations with Spielberger's State-Trait Anxiety Inventory have been low to

149

moderate (-.13 to -.65). The correlations among the items comprising a given score have generally been low, suggesting that the items do not measure a single characteristic.

Scoring & Interpretation

Scoring is moderately complex and time consuming. For each item, the manual lists several examples of responses that are to be scored positively, several that are to be scored negatively, several that are to be scored as neutral, and several that the student should be asked to further clarify. Studies suggest that most adults can be trained to properly score the instrument within four hours. Norms based on 4,412 Air Force recruits are reported.

Comments

The instrument is adult in content and tone. No reading is required, the administrator orally presents the beginning of each sentence. The student is supposed to write his or her response after giving it orally, but there appears to be no reason why the administrator could not do that.

A 1985 review (in The Ninth Mental Measurements Yearbook, #153) concluded that this instrument is suitable for assessing the psychopathology of everyday life.

Availability

The publisher might restrict distribution of this instrument to researchers and psychologists.

Price

Thirty copies of the instrument cost $25.00. The manual, which includes a copy of the instrument, costs $13.00.

Source

Stoelting
1350 South Kostner Ave.
Chicago, IL 60623-1196
(312) 522-4500

California Psychological Inventory (CPI)

Author & Date

Harrison G. Gough (1956-1987)

Purpose

To assess normal personality characteristics that are important in everyday life.

Description

The instrument is comprised of 462 statements about oneself. The student is to indicate whether each statement is "true" or "false." The statements are like: "I am as ambitious as most other people;" "My life is boring;" and "I seldom become angry." Twenty scores are generated from the responses. They are for dominance, capacity for status, sociability, social presence, self-acceptance, independence, empathy, responsibility, socialization, self-control, good impression, communality, sense of well-being, tolerance, achievement via conformance, achievement via independence, intellectual efficiency, psychological mindedness, flexibility, femininity/masculinity.

Administration

The instrument can be administered individually or to a group. The instructions are clear and simple. There is no time limit. The manual says most persons complete it within 60 minutes, but low-literate respondents would probably need more time because of the large number of items.

Alternate Forms

Translations of an earlier version of the instrument into several languages have been used extensively, but the publisher does not sell them.

Reliability

Test-retest correlations for each of the twenty scores were mostly moderate (.5 to .75) in a sample of high school students with a one year interval. Internal reliability, measured by alpha coefficients was mostly moderate or high (.55 to .85) for a sample of college students.

Validity

Numerous validity studies have been conducted. They generally have yielded low and moderate correlations (.25 to .6). Many of the correlations among the individual scores of the CPI are moderate (.5 to .75), indicating that they are measures of characteristics that are not independent of each other.

Scoring & Interpretation

Scoring is relatively simple, but time-consuming because of the large number of items measuring 20 different characteristics. There is a separate scoring template for each of the 20 characteristics. Each template is placed on the answer sheet, the number of responses that show through the template are counted. The raw scores are recorded on profile sheets. Computerized scoring is available from the publisher. There are norm data based on several thousand persons, including 4,162 high school students, 3,236 college students, and small samples of persons employed in eleven different professional occupations.

Comments

This instrument was designed for persons age 14 and older. It requires reading at about the 6th grade level. The large number of items is likely to be daunting to many adults with limited literacy skills. The CPI is one of the most widely used personality assessment tools. It was revised in 1986, for the first time in thirty years. Eighteen items were eliminated, and 29 were modified to reflect current language, simplify the wording, and reduce biases. Two new scores, independence and empathy were added. Scores from the revised version correlate .91 or higher with those from the original one.

There have been numerous reviews of the instrument. They have judged it to be anywhere from decent to very good. Its strengths are a focus on social behavior rather than esoteric personality traits. Its weaknesses are low to moderate validity coefficients, but most experts think that is about all that can be achieved when measuring broad behavioral tendencies with a questionnaire. One of the leading textbooks on measurement (Essentials of Psychological Testing, 4th Edition) concluded, "Used by trained and cautious counselors, CPI serves screening and descriptive purposes as well as any questionnaire." A 1985 review (in the Ninth Mental Measurements Yearbook, #182) concluded that the CPI is not a perfect, but its critics have not been able to suggest a superior instrument for the same purpose.

Availability

This instrument is only available to professionals with: 1) training or experience in the use of tests, and 2) completion of an advance degree in an appropriate profession, membership in a relevant professional association, or a state license in psychology.

Price

Twenty-five reusable booklets cost $18.75. Fifty answer sheets cost $6.00. A specimen set with a copy of the administrator's guide costs $17.00. Computerized scoring costs $3.25 per answer sheet when 10 to 50 are submitted at one time.

Source

Consulting Psychologists Press
577 College Avenue
Palo Alto, CA 94306
(415) 857-1444

Coopersmith Self-Esteem Inventory (SEI)

Author & Date
Stanley Coopersmith (1967-1981)

Purpose
To measure the evaluations a person makes of himself or herself, especially in the areas of social, academic, family, and personal functioning.

Description
The instrument consists of brief self-description statements. The respondent is to indicate whether each is "like me" or "unlike me." The form for adults has 25 statements like: "People can depend on me" and "I am not as smart most others. The material given to the students is called the "Coopersmith Inventory," with no mention of self-esteem.

Administration
The instrument can be administered individually or to a group. The instructions are simple and clear. For students with weaker reading skills, the administrator is to read each item aloud. There is no time limit. Most students should finish in less than ten minutes.

Alternate Forms
In addition to the adult form, there are long and short student forms (58 and 25 statements)

Reliability
Test-retest reliability for the long student form was high (.88) after a five week interval and moderate (.70) after a three year interval. Test-retest reliability for the short student form was high (.80 to .82) for college students after an unspecified interval. KR-20 has generally been high (.80 to .90) for the long student form, but would undoubtedly be somewhat lower for the shorter adult form.

Validity
A study of 7600 school children by Kokenes (1974, 1978) "confirmed the construct validity of the subscales proposed by Coopersmith." Several other studies, reported in the manual, correlated the scores on the student form with those of other self-concept questionnaires, achievement, and behavioral ratings. The correlations were generally

low to moderate (mostly .3 to .6). This evidence is also applicable to the adult form because most of the items on the adult form are taken from the student form, some verbatim and some with slight wording changes.

Scoring & Interpretation

Scoring is simple and quick. An answer key indicates the high self-esteem responses. They are counted and multiplied by four. The mean scores from eleven studies are reported in the manual. The means for subgroups (male/female, racial/ethnic groups, and various grade levels) are also reported. Only one study of adults is included, but the other studies show only very small differences between the lowest and highest school grades. These data can be aggregated and used as a rough estimate of national norms.

Comments

The Coopersmith SEI is among the best known and most widely used of the various self-esteem measures. About a 4th grade reading level is required.

Seventeen of the twenty-five items are negative descriptions. Some students in adult literacy programs may feel that the instrument is trying to negatively stereotype them. Most instruments reviewed in this section use both negative and positive descriptions, but not such a high proportion of the former.

A 1984 textbook on human measurement (Essentials of Psychological Testing, 4th Edition), described this instrument as a "workaday instrument," but notes that students can easily fake high esteem on it.

Availability

The instrument is restricted to persons who have completed courses in tests and measurements at a university or have received equivalent documented training.

Price

Twenty-five non-reusable forms cost $3.50. A specimen set including a copy of the manual costs $6.50.

Source

Consulting Psychologists Press
577 College Avenue
Palo Alto, CA 94306
(415) 857-1444

Culture-Free Self Esteem Inventories

Author & Date
James Battle (1981)

Purpose
To measure an individual's perception of self.

Description
There are 40 self-description questions. The student marks "yes" if the question "describes how you usually feel," and "no" if it "does not describe how you usually feel." The questions are like: "Are you as smart as most other people?" and "Do most people like you?" There are five scores: general self esteem, social self-esteem, personal self-esteem, total, and lying.

Administration
The instrument can be administered individually or to a group. The instructions are simple and clear. There is no time limit. Most students finish within 20 minutes. For beginning readers, pre-recorded cassettes in English, Spanish, and French are available for administering the instrument orally.

Alternate Forms
There is just one adult form, Form AD. There is also a long children's form (60 items), Form A, and a short children's form (30 items), Form B. Each form is also available in French and Spanish, as well as English.

Reliability
Test-retest reliability, after an unspecified period, has been moderate to high (.56 to .82) for the three scores of general, social, and personal self-esteem, and high (.82) for the total. KR-20 has been moderate (.57 to .78) for the scores of general, social, and personal self-esteem.

Validity
The manual reports moderately high correlations (.71 to .82) between the children's form of the instrument and the Coopersmith Self-Esteem Inventory. But there are enough differences between that form and the adult form to make those results of limited use in judging the validity of the latter. Several case studies of low self-esteem individuals in psychotherapy have found substantial increases in the scores on this instrument as the therapy progressed. In a job preparation program for unemployed

young adults that included components to alleviate low self-esteem and depression, there were substantial increases in each of the scores on the adult form. In two studies, the total score on this instrument correlated moderately with measures of depression (-.55 to -.75), and that is the same relation found between other measures of self-esteem and depression. The correlations between the general, social, and personal self-esteem have been low and moderately low (.15 to .54), indicating that they do measure reasonably different characteristics. Factor analyses confirm that the individual items have been reasonably assigned to the specific score they are used to calculate.

Scoring & Interpretation

Manual scoring is simple and quick. Computerized scoring is available from the publisher. Very limited norm data are reported for 252 adults. The manual does not describe any characteristics of those adults, but it appears that at least half were Canadian college students.

Comments

The adult form of this inventory was developed specifically for adults. Required reading, when the instrument is not administered orally, is at about the fifth grade level. A 1985 review (in The Ninth Mental Measurements Yearbook, #291) found there was no evidence that the instrument is actually culture-free, as suggested by its name.

One advantage of this instrument, compared to most other measures of self-esteem reviewed in this section, is that it has a means of detecting when students are faking answers.

This reviewer has substantial experience administering the instrument to adult literacy students. In five of nine sites some students exhibited moderate to substantial displeasure with several of the items. They expressed distaste for questions that asked them to compare themselves with others; complained that the questions focused on the negative and were trying to stereotype them (14 of the questions are about positive characteristics and 26 are about negative ones); correctly identified the purpose of some of the lie scale items; ridiculed ambiguity in the wording of a few items; and expressed frustration with having to answer "Yes" or "No" to the questions (many, but not all, questions include a qualifier like "usually" or "seldom"). The most offensive items were not the ones that measure self-esteem, but rather the ones used to detect faked answers. The two most objectionable items asked the students if they have ever engaged in common acts of dishonesty. At four other sites, however, the instrument provoked only a few nervous chuckles. In one of those four, the students afterwards told the teacher that several of the questions addressed important issues in their lives and asked to discuss those issues in class. Several hypotheses for the differing reactions were examined, but no explanation could be found.

Ironically, the instrument found substantial gains in self-esteem at several of the sites, including those where there had been adverse reactions to it.

Availability

The instrument will be sold to anyone.

Price

Twenty-five non-reusable instruments cost $6.00. The manual costs $12.50. A specimen set, including a copy of the manual, costs $15.00.

Source

Special Child Publications
P.O. Box 33548
Seattle, WA 98133
(206) 771-5711

The Facial Interpersonal Perception Inventory (FIPI)

Author & Date J

Joseph J. Luciani and Richard E. Carney (1980)

Purpose

To measure self-perception and ideal self.

Description

The instrument consists of thirteen simple cartoon faces with different expressions. The student is asked to mark the number beside each face that best shows how well the face shows "the way I see myself now." The numbers range from 1 to 7, with the former indicating "least" like myself, and the latter indicating "most" like myself. Then the student is asked to answer again in respect to "the way I would like to be." The instrument focuses on pleasant or unpleasant affect, open or closed to incoming information, and relaxed or tense. There are scores for each of these characteristics for one's self, for incongruence between ideal and actual self, and for various inconsistencies.

Administration

The instructions are simple, but there is a problem in clarity that is mentioned below in the section on "Validity." For students with no reading skills or very low reading skills, the instrument can be administered individually with verbal instructions. Students with more than a 6th grade reading ability are able to self-administer the instrument by reading the short instructions and then rating each cartoon face. There is no time limit; most students should complete the instrument in less than five minutes.

Alternate Forms

None. The manual states that the instrument can be administered verbally in languages other than English, but instructions and answer sheets in other languages are not provided.

Reliability

Test-retest reliability of the three self-perception scores is moderate to high (.64 to .94). The other scores were not subjected to this analysis.

Validity

There is considerable data in the section of the manual that is titled "Validity," but little of it is directly relevant to the validity of this instrument. Most of the correlations are with other instruments that do not measure the characteristics that this instrument tries to assess.

There is a potential problem with the rating scale. Each face is supposed to be individually rated on the extent to which it is "least" or "most" like the way I see myself. In common English usage, "least" and "most" are terms used to express a relative relationship among two or more options. On this instrument, however, the different faces are not supposed to be compared; instead, each one is supposed to be rated separately. Proper English usage would have labeled the extremities of the rating scale as "not at all like me" and "very much like me."

Scoring & Interpretation

Hand scoring involves 79 computations! Computerized scoring is available from the publisher. No norm data are provided.

Comments

The aspects of self-image that this instrument attempts to assess are limited. They center on happiness, open-mindedness, and anxiety. Self-esteem, sense of efficacy, and self-confidence are not addressed. The instrument was developed for children, and looks childish. Some adults might find it demeaning.

Two 1985 reviews (Ninth Mental Measurements Yearbook, #407) found this to be an intriguing instrument, but with little evidence about whether it actually measures self-image. The manual that is currently being distributed was prepared in 1980, is marked "Rough First Draft" and is incomplete.

Availability

This instrument will be sold to anyone.

Price

Fifty copies of the non-reusable booklet cost $12.00. A specimen set, including the manual, costs $7.00.

Source

Carney Weedman and Associates
4776 El Cajon Blvd. #203
San Diego, CA 92115
(619) 582-2005

Gordon Personal Profile-Inventory (GPP-I)

Author & Date

Leonard V. Gordon (1951-78)

Purpose

To measure certain personality traits that are significant in the daily functioning of individuals.

Description

There are 38 items. Each is comprised of four descriptive statements. The student is to indicate which statement is most like him or her and which is least like him or her. An example is: "has an excellent appetite, gets sick very often, follows a well-balanced diet, doesn't get enough exercise." There are nine scores--for responsibility, emotional stability, sociability, ascendancy, self-esteem (a composite of the prior four scores), original thinking, cautiousness, vigor, and personal relations.

Administration

The instrument can be administered individually or to a group. The instructions are simple and clear, but following them is intellectually complex for reasons discussed below in the "Comments." There is no time limit. Most students take 20 to 30 minutes.

Alternate Forms

This instrument is really a combination of two others, the Gordon Personal Profile which yields the first five scores listed above, and the Gordon Personal Inventory which yields the last four scores listed above. Each of those instruments is also available individually.

Reliability

Test-retest reliability of the individual scores has been low to moderate (mostly between .45 to .70). Split-half reliability has been high (.80 to .89). The self-esteem score has exhibited higher reliability, which is to be expected since it is the total of four scores.

Validity

Correlations between individual scores on this instrument and peer, counselor, or superiors' ratings have been low to moderate (.21 to .73). Correlations between the individual scores on this instrument and comparable scores on the Eysenck Personality Inventory and on the Guilford-Zimmerman Temperament Survey have generally been moderate (mostly .50 to .65). The correlations between the self-esteem score from this instrument and the Coopersmith Self-Esteem Inventory have been moderately high (.74 to .77) in a sample of college students. Several studies have examined the extent to which students are likely to fake positive responses to the instrument. The results suggest there is more faking when taking the instrument during employment applications than when taking it for guidance purposes, but the faking is limited, on the average, to only about two points on each score. Several studies have examined scores on this instrument for different racial and ethnic groups. Once socioeconomic level and occupation are controlled for, there are few differences, they are small in magnitude, and not consistent from study to study.

Scoring & Interpretation

Scoring is moderately simple. It takes about five minutes per instrument. There are national norms for 6,534 male sophomores and 2,422 female sophomores--at moderately and highly selective colleges. There are norms for about 4,000 male high school students and 4,000 female high school students in the northeastern and midwestern parts of the country. Scores are also reported for samples of adults in many different occupations.

Comments

This instrument has been used in more than 200 published studies. It is adult in content and tone.

The required reading is at about the seventh grade level when judged by the vocabulary and length of sentences. A peculiarity in the wording of the items, however, makes their comprehension quite difficult. The problem is caused by the use of double and triple negatives. Some of the descriptive statements begin with "lacking," "does not" or "not too," creating a first level of negative; some of the trailing parts of the statements are negative, creating the second level; then the instruction to select the statement "least like you" is a third level of negative. As a result, sometimes the student is forced to select, as least like him or her, among: a positive trait, a negative trait, a not positive trait, and a not negative trait. This reviewer found it intellectually demanding to answer the items--even though he scored well on the critical thinking tests reviewed in the next section of this book.

Availability

This test will be sold to professional evaluators; appropriate administrators of accredited schools, colleges, and government agencies; and to organizations where the instrument's use will be supervised by person with at least a Masters degree in psychology or a related discipline and appropriate training in measurement.

Price

Thirty-five non-reusable student booklets and the manual cost $70.00. A specimen set, including a copy of the manual, costs $30.00.

Source

The Psychological Corporation
555 Academic Court
San Antonio, TX 78204-0952
(512) 299-1061

Interpersonal Style Inventory
(ISI)

Author & Date

Maurice Lorr & Richard Youniss (1972-86)

Purpose

To measure an individual's ways of relating to other persons, work, and play.

Description

The instrument has 300 self-descriptive statements. The statements are like: "I want other people's advice before making decisions;" "I say what I think, even when I know others will disagree;" and "Once I start something, I usually finish it." The student marks each as true (if is "true or mostly true") or false (if it is "false or not usually true"). There are fifteen scores: sociable, help-seeking (vs. self-sufficient), nurturing (altruistic, benevolent), sensitive, conscientious, trusting, directive, independent, rule-free (unconventional and individualistic), deliberate, orderly, persistent, stable (vs. anxious when under stress), and approval seeking (fakes good impressions). There are also several checks for validity of responses.

Administration

The instrument can be administered individually or to a group. The instructions are simple and clear. There is no time limit. The manual says most students finish within 50 minutes, but limited readers will probably need more time because of the large number of items.

Alternate Forms

There is only one form.

Reliability

Test-retest reliability over a two week interval has been high (.80 to .95). Internal reliability measured by coefficient alpha has been moderate to high (.72 to .89).

Validity

Correlations of the scores with comparable ones on the Orientation and Motivation Inventory have been mostly moderate and high (.52 to .88). Correlations with self-ratings and peer-ratings have been mostly low to moderate (.30 to .75). Scores on earlier versions of this instrument have correlated with comparable scores on the 16 Personality Factors Questionnaire, the Edwards Personal Preference Schedule, the

Personality Research Form, and the Comrey Personality Scale mostly at low and moderate levels (.25 to .60). Items with high social-desirability bias were screened out during development of the instrument. Most of the scores have low correlations (less than .50) with the other scores on the instrument, indicating that there is relatively little overlap in the characteristics being measured.

Scoring & Interpretation

Scoring cannot be done manually. Computerized scoring is done by the publisher. It is expensive--$6.00 per person when 6-24 answer sheets are submitted at one time. There are norms based on 647 high school students in five diverse neighborhoods of Baltimore, and based on 765 college students from twelve diverse institutions. There are separate norms for males and females, because there are significant average differences between them on several of the scores.

Comments

This instrument is adult in content and tone. The required reading is at about the 7th grade level. It uses some common slang words, such as "jam" and "cool," which gives it an informal feeling. Some adult literacy students may balk at having to complete such a large number of items.

A 1985 review (in The Ninth Mental Measurements Yearbook, #521) concluded that the instrument compares favorably with other highly sophisticated inventories of personal characteristics.

Availability

This instrument is sold only to "qualified professional users."

Price

Ten reusable student booklets cost $16.50. Answer sheets, with pre-paid computerized scoring, cost $6.00 each in batches of 6-24, and $5.45 each in batches of 25-99. The manual costs $18.50.

Source

Western Psychological Services
12031 Wilshire Blvd.
Los Angeles, CA 90025
(800) 222-2670, or (800) 423-7863 in California

Jackson Personality Inventory
(JPI)

Author & Date

Douglas N. Jackson (1971-84)

Purpose

To measure a variety of interpersonal, cognitive, and value orientations likely to have important implication for a person's functioning.

Description

There are 320 self-description statements. The student is to respond to each by indicating whether it is true or false, "even if you are not completely sure of your answer." The statements are like: "I am a solid, reliable type of person;" "I'll say what I believe even when I know others will disagree;" "I am saddened by other people's misfortunes." There are fifteen personality scores: Anxiety, Breadth of Interest, Complexity (contemplative, discerning, and analytical), Conformity, Energy Level, Innovation, Interpersonal Affect (kind, compassionate), Organization, Responsibility, Risk Taking, Self-Esteem, Social Adroitness (shrewd, tactful, and persuasive) Social Participation (gregarious, congenial, good natured), Tolerance, and Value Orthodoxy.

Administration

The instrument can be administered individually or to a group. The instructions are simple and clear. There is no time limit. The manual says that most students finish within sixty minutes, but many limited readers will probably need longer because of the large number of items.

Alternate Forms

There is just one form.

Reliability

Test-retest reliability is not reported in the manual. Internal consistency, calculated by Bentler's Theta, has ranged from .75 to .95.

Validity

Correlations of the scores from this instrument with comparable scores from other instruments, including the Bentler Psychological Inventory, the Bentler Interactive Psychological Inventory, and the Minnesota Multiphasic Personality Inventory have generally been moderate (mostly .4 to .75). Correlations with peer ratings of the same

166

characteristics have generally been low (mostly .15 to .5). Correlations with self-ratings have generally been moderate (mostly .4 to .75). Correlations between the scores and a measure of social desirability response bias (marking answers the way one thinks is desirable) have been low.

Scoring & Interpretation

Scoring is simple, but takes about five minutes because of the large number of items. Norm data are based on 2,000 male and 2,000 female students from a random sample of 43 North American colleges.

Comments

This instrument was developed for adults. The required reading is at about the seventh grade level.

A 1978 review (in The Eighth Mental Measurements Yearbook, #593) challenged the appropriateness of many items and noted that some items are likely to be frustrating because neither a "Yes" or "No" response to them will be accurate. Another 1978 review (in the same source) judged the manual for the instrument to be deficient, but highly recommended the instrument for research purposes. A 1984 textbook (Essentials of Psychological Testing) says the instrument has been praised for its painstaking construction.

Availability

This instrument will be sold only to those who have completed an advanced level university course in psychological measurement or have received such training from a qualified psychologist.

Price

Twenty-five reusable student booklets cost $19.00. Twenty-five answer sheets cost $4.75. The manual costs $8.50. An examination kit with ten copies of the student booklets and answer sheets, and one copy of the manual, costs $27.50.

Source

Research Psychologist Press
P.O. Box 984
Port Huron, MI 48061-0984
(800) 265-1285

The Schutz Measures--Element S: Self-Concept

Author & Date
Will Schutz (1982-1983)

Purpose
To measure how a person feels about himself or herself.

Description
There are 54 statements about oneself. The statements are like: "I feel good about myself;" "I often feel like I am in a haze;" and "I trust myself to do well." The student is asked to respond to each on a six-point scale. The number 1 represents "definitely not true," and 6 represents "especially true." The student is to mark the number that best describes his or her "present feelings or behavior." Then the student is asked to go through the statements again and indicate "the way you would like to feel or be." Six scores are computed from each set of responses. They are: ability to concentrate, self-control, awareness, feelings of significance, feelings of competency, liking of oneself.

Administration
The instrument can be self-administered. It also can be administered individually and to groups. The instructions are simple and straight-forward. There is no time limit. Most students will need 10 to 20 minutes.

Alternate Forms
None.

Reliability
Test-retest reliability is not reported in the manual. Internal consistency has been high (.88 to .97).

Validity
No validity data are presented in the manual. The publisher states that because the instrument is similar to the thoroughly studied Fundamental Interpersonal Relations Orientation (FIRO) scales it can be presumed to have similar statistical properties. When revising or deriving instruments from existing ones, normal professional practice is to empirically compare the results from administration of the old and new instruments to a sample of persons. This apparently has not been done.

The answer sheet for this instrument is different from that used with the FIRO and not common in professional measurement. A heavy line is placed over the responses that are to be counted as high self-concept. This permits scoring without a template or separate answer key. Heavy lines are also placed under some items, including a few with overhead lines, to disguise the purpose of the overhead lines. When students ask about the heavy lines, they are told to disregard them. But it is possible that the lines influence some student's responses, and there is no data presented in the manual indicating that this is not the case.

Scoring & Interpretation

Manual scoring is moderately simple. Each of the scores is just the count of all designated responses in a row on the answer sheet. Twelve rows need to be counted. Difference scores are then calculated by subtracting the scores for the ideal self from the scores for actual self. The manual presents norm data by age and sex for a sample of 200 persons, most of whom were college students.

Comments

The required reading is at about the seventh grade level. The response sheet is separate from the sheet with the statements to which the student is to respond, and has a different layout. Some ESL and low reading native-born students are likely to be confused about where to mark their answers.

Availability

This instrument is restricted to persons who have completed courses in tests and measurements at a university or have received equivalent documented training.

Price

Twenty-five reusable booklets cost $7.75. Fifty answer sheets and interpretive guides cost $15.00. A specimen set with a copy of the manual costs $9.00 and includes three other related instruments.

Source

Consulting Psychologists Press
577 College Avenue
Palo Alto, CA 94306
(415) 857-1444

Self-Concept Evaluation of Location Form (SELF)

Author & Date
Richard E. Carney and others (1978-80)

Purpose
To assess the structure of self-concept.

Description
Sixteen pairs of opposite words are separated by a seven point scale. The words are like: "neat and sloppy," "smart and dumb," "honest and dishonest." The student is to indicate what point on the scale best describes "the way I see myself now." Then the same words and scales are repeated and the student is to indicate "the way I would like to be." The sixteen items yield scores for goodness, potency and activity, self concept (an aggregate of the former three), the incongruence between the present and ideal perceptions, and various inconsistencies.

Administration
The instrument can be administered to individuals or groups. There is no time limit, but it generally should not take more than ten minutes.

Alternate Forms
There is only one form.

Reliability
Test-retest reliability is not reported except for a series of studies in which the instrument was used in a non-standard way. Split half reliability has been high (.83).

Validity
The SELF was validated against the Tennessee Self-Concept Scale--a widely used and generally well respected instrument. The scores for goodness, potency, and activity correlated moderately (.455 to .658) with the total positive scores on the Tennessee for a sample of college students. Correlations between the SELF incongruence and inconsistency and the Tennessee "Net Conflict," Total Conflict," and "Total Variance" were low (none exceeded .32).

Scoring & Interpretation

Complete manual scoring involves a maze of 88 computations. But manual scoring of the basic self-concept score involves only one computation and can be done in a minute. Computerized scoring is available from the publisher. Norm data are given for total positive self-concept and for total incongruence. These data are apparently from a sample of 175 college students and 64 junior high school students in southern California during the late 1970s. Data are also presented for small samples of neurotics, psychotics, and psychopaths. They differed only moderately on total positive self-concept from the norm population, but had substantially greater total incongruence.

Comments

This instrument was designed for adolescents and adults. The required reading is at about the fifth grade level.

When the students have very limited experience with paper and pencil instruments, the administrator probably should demonstrate answering the example problem on the cover sheet rather than just having the students work it. This minor departure in the instructions is unlikely to affect the responses, except to avoid some misunderstandings that would not have occurred with the norm population.

A 1985 review (in the Ninth Mental Measurements Yearbook, #1093) concluded the Tennessee Self-Concept Scale is preferred to the SELF if measures of discrete aspects of self-concept (such as moral self, social self, and family self) are desired.

This reviewer thinks there is considerable evidence that the total positive self-concept score and the total incongruence score of the SELF are valid measures of what they aim to measure. The instrument can be administered very quickly and the former score requires only one computation. The Tennessee can provide more detailed information, but it takes longer to administer (20 minutes versus about 5 minutes) and has some limitations of its own.

Availability

This instrument will be sold to anyone.

Price

Fifty non-reusable booklets cost $12.50. A specimen set with a copy of the manual costs $7.50. Computerized scoring by the publisher costs $1.00 per booklet.

Source

Carney Weedman and Associates
4776 El Cajon Blvd. #203
San Diego, CA 92115
(619) 582-2005

Self-Description Inventory

Author & Date
Charles B. Johansson (1975-83)

Purpose
To measure individual differences along normal personality dimensions and vocational dimensions.

Description
The instrument is comprised of 200 self-descriptive adjectives. The adjectives are like: "brave," "excitable," and "prudent." The student codes each as "Yes" if the adjective is always or usually true of himself or herself, as "Sometimes" if it is sometimes true or if he or she is uncertain, and as "No" if it is not true or rarely true. Eleven personality scores and vocational orientation scores are computed. The personality scores are: cautious/adventurous, nonscientific/analytical; tense/relaxed, insecure/confident, conventional/imaginative, impatient/patient, unconcerned/altruistic, reserved/outgoing, soft-spoken/forceful, lackadaisical/industrious, and unorganized/orderly. The vocational orientation scores are: realistic, investigative, artistic, social, enterprising, and conventional.

Administration
The instrument can be administered individually or to a group. The instructions are simple and clear. There is no time limit. Most students take 15 to 20 minutes.

Alternate Forms
There is only one form.

Reliability
Test-retest reliability after one and two weeks has been moderate to high (.70 to .94). Split-half reliability has been moderate to high (.59 to .90).

Validity
Correlations with similar scores on the Omnibus Personality Inventory, Myers-Briggs Type Indicator, and Minnesota Multiphasic Personality Inventory have been generally moderate (.40 to .70). The mean scores of persons satisfied with their work in various occupations has been generally as expected. For instance, firemen score much higher on adventurousness than do librarians, authors score much higher on imagination than

do security guards, child care workers score much higher on altruism than do machinists.

Scoring & Interpretation

The instrument is available only with prepaid computerized scoring by the publisher. The scoring is normally completed within 24 hours of receipt.

There are norms for adolescents, young adults age 20 to 25 (half of whom were in college or vocational training), and adults age 26-55 (almost all of whom were employed). The norms are based on a total of 1,878 people, of whom 93 percent were caucasian. An analysis of racial differences among students at five community colleges was conducted. The results indicated that minority males differed significantly from caucasian males by feeling moderately more relaxed, confident, and altruistic. There were no significant differences among the females.

Comments

This instrument was designed for adolescents and adults. Though some of the adjectives are clearly negative characteristics, most are neutral or positive. Most are not threatening and not emotionally laden.

A reading level of about the eighth grade level is required. The manual states that the instrument can be administered orally to students of lower reading skill, but some of the adjectives involve sophisticated vocabulary that will not be understood by many students, whether read or presented orally.

Two 1985 reviews (in The Ninth Mental Measurements Yearbook, #1096) concluded that this is a good instrument--well constructed and well validated.

Availability

The instrument is available to professional evaluators, school and college officials, and those with a psychology degree or closely related degree who can document course work in psychological assessment.

Price

The instrument is only sold with pre-paid computer scoring included. In quantities of 5-29 the price is $4.00 each; in quantities over 100 it is $2.80 each. The manual costs $10.25. A specimen set, including a copy of the manual and a copy of the instrument that may be returned for free scoring, costs $12.50.

Source

National Computer Systems
P.O. Box 1416
Minneapolis, MN 55440
(800) 328-6759, or (612) 933-2800 in Minnesota

Self-Directed Learning Readiness Scale (SDLRS)

Author & Date

Lucy M. Guglielmino (1977-88)

Purpose

To assess a person's readiness for self-directed learning.

Description

The instrument has 58 self-descriptive statements. The student responds on a five-point scale with 1="I never feel like this" and 5="I feel like this all the time." The statements are like: "I like to learn," "I have many questions about things," and "I work well by myself." There is just one score, the total.

Administration

The instrument can be administered individually or to a group. The instructions are simple and clear. The self-descriptive statements can be read aloud to the students, and one study found that oral administration and oral responses did not affect the average scores. There is no time limit.

Alternate Forms

There are several forms of this instrument. Form A is for the general adult population. Form ABE is for adults of low reading levels and for non-native speakers of English.

Reliability

Test-retest reliability is not reported in the materials provided by the publisher. Internal consistency has been high (.77 to .87).

Validity

One study found a correlation between scores on Form A of this instrument and students' self-reports on the number of learning projects they had undertaken. A second study found no relation between the scores and faculty members' ratings of college students' self-directedness, but the faculty members had limited knowledge of the students' lives. A third study found a correlation between scores on Form A of this instrument and grades in a nursing courses that relied on a high level of self-direction by the students (the magnitude of the correlations is not reported). The ABE form is very similar to Form A (see "Comments" below), and thus is likely to exhibit similar validity.

Scoring & Interpretation

Manual scoring is simple and quick. Computerized scoring is available. Limited norms, based on 151 Adult Basic Education students in three states, are available.

Comments

The ABE form of this instrument, for low reading adults and non-native speakers of English, is new. But it is quite similar to Form A, an earlier form of the instrument developed for the general adult population. The main differences are some rewording to lower the required reading level to about the fourth grade level, and elimination of idioms and grammatical structures that might pose problems for non-native speakers of English.

This instrument is described as assessing "abilities, attitudes, and personality characteristics related to self-directed learning." It should be noted that the assessment of abilities is limited to the student's perceptions of his or her abilities to learn by his or herself. There are no questions that measure a student's actual knowledge of learning resources or skill in using them.

Availability

This instrument will be sold to anyone.

Price

The cost is $3.00 per person for a student booklet, answer sheet, and computer scoring. That charge declines to $2.50 for 50-200 persons. A manual had not been prepared at the time of this review, but the author had written a paper describing the development of Form ABE.

Source

Guglielmino and Associates
734 Marble Way
Boca Raton, FL 33432
(305) 392-0379

Self-Esteem Questionnaire
(SEQ-3)

Author & Date
James K. Hoffmeister (1971-76)

Purpose
To assess one's sense of his or her capability, significance, success, and worth; also to assess one's satisfaction with his or her sense of these characteristics.

Description
There are a twelve statements about a person's self-perceptions and others' regard for the person. The statements are like: "I usually make good decisions;" and "Most people want me for a friend." Following nine of those statements there is a question, "Does the situation described in number ... upset you?" The multiple-choice responses for both the statements and the questions are: "Not at all," "Only a little," "Depends or Not sure," "Pretty much," and "Yes, very much." There are two scores. The one for self-esteem is based on responses to the statements. The one for self-other satisfaction is based on the responses to the questions.

Administration
The instrument can be administered individually or to a group. The instructions are moderately simple and clear. There is no time limit; most students finish within 5 minutes.

Alternate Forms
There is only one form.

Reliability
Test-retest reliability with 4th, 5th, and 6th graders, after a two week interval has been moderate ("about .70") for each of the two scores. Internal reliability, measured by Cronbach's alpha, has been high (.80 to .96).

Validity
The correlation of the self-esteem score on this instrument and the total score on the Coopersmith Self-Esteem Inventory (short form for children) has been moderate (.61). The correlation of the self-other satisfaction score with the Coopersmith has been moderately low (.40). Those results were for 225 5th graders. The correlations between scores on this instrument and parent and teacher ratings of students' self

esteem has be low ("about .30"). There have not been significant differences between males and females, or among different racial/ethnic groups on either score.

Scoring & Interpretation

Manual scoring is moderately simple and quick. The scores for the self-esteem items are totalled (a few have to be reversed first), and then divided by 12. The scores for the self-other satisfaction items are totalled and then divided by 9. Computerized scoring is available from the publisher. Limited norm data are given for elementary school students, junior and senior high school students, and adults. There is also data on students at the elementary, junior high, and senior high level who have a history of reading difficulties.

Comments

This instrument apparently was developed for use with youth, but the content and tone are adult. The required reading is at about the fifth grade level. The instrument is printed on a computer scannable form with many tiny rectangles to be filled in. It could be confusing and intimidating to ESL students and very low-level native born students.

The statements in this instrument seem to measure three types of perceptions. Some of the perceptions are about one's self, some of the perceptions are about one's self in comparison to others, and some of the perceptions are about other's thoughts and feelings toward one's self. The latter is sometimes referred to in other instruments as "reflected esteem" rather than "self-esteem."

The instrument is labeled at the top as "Self-Esteem Questionnaire." The instructions printed on the back of the instrument begin by defining self-esteem. This is not good practice. If the students know what is being assessed, they are more prone to give whatever they perceive to be the desired or good responses.

A 1978 review (in The Eighth Mental Measurements Yearbook, #672) questioned the unusual computerized scoring procedure of this instrument (but not the manual scoring procedure) and concluded that there is limited data on how the instrument performs.

Availability

The instrument will be sold to anyone.

Price

Each copy of the instrument, which includes an answer sheet, costs $0.25. The manual, including a copy of the instrument, costs $10.00.

Source

Test Analysis and Development Corporation
2400 Park Lake Drive
Boulder, CO 80301
(303) 666-8651

Self-Observation Scales
(SOS)

Author & Date
Jackson Stenner & William G. Katzenmeyer (1974-79)

Purpose
To measure several dimensions of self-image.

Description
The student responds with "yes" or "no" to a series of self-descriptive statements. The statements are like: "I am a happy person;" "This school stinks;" and "People like me." There are 50 to 72 items, depending on the level of the instrument. The lowest level of the instrument, for students in grades K-3, has scores for self acceptance, self security, social maturity, and school affiliation. The highest level of the instrument has the following seven scores: self acceptance, self security, social confidence, self assertion, peer affiliation, teacher affiliation, and school affiliation.

Administration
The instrument can be administered individually or to a group. The instructions are simple and clear. There is no time limit. Most students finish in 20 to 30 minutes.

Alternate Forms
There are four levels of the instrument, "Primary Level" for grades K-3, "Intermediate Level" for grades 4-6, "Junior High Level" for grades 7-9, and Senior High Level" for grades 10-12. There are two forms for the first and second level, and one for the third and forth level.

Reliability
Test-retest reliability of the scores has been moderately high (.73 to .91). Split-half reliability has been moderate to high (.56 to .86).

Validity
The manual does not report studies correlating the scores of this instrument with those of other measures of self-image. It does, however, report studies of the correlations between scores on this instrument and measures of academic achievement. Studies in elementary schools have shown low to moderate correlations (.39 to .50). Other statistical analyses suggest that the scores measure the same underlying factors in bilingual Latino children as they do in other American children.

Scoring & Interpretation

This instrument is only sold with pre-paid computerized scoring by the publisher. The reports indicate how given scores compare with national norms based on several thousand persons.

Comments

This instrument was designed specifically for school children in grades K-12. With an important exception, the content and tone of the Junior High and Senior High levels of the instrument is appropriate for adults. The exception is that about one-third of the items refer to "my teachers" and "my school." For adults who are in a part-time instructional programs, especially ones that strive not to be like "school," these questions could be confusing and irrelevant. A reading level of about the sixth grade is needed for the Junior High and Senior High versions of the instrument.

Availability

This instrument is sold to anyone.

Price

Thirty answer sheets, the Administration Manual, and pre-paid computerized scoring cost $50.00. The Technical Manual costs $5.00. A specimen set, including a copy of the technical manual, costs $10.95.

Source

NTS Research Corporation
209 Markham Dr.
Chapel Hill, NC 27514
(919) 942-7551

Self-Perception Inventory (SPI)

Author & Date

Anthony T. Soares and Louise M. Soares (1965-1985)

Purpose

To measure people's perceptions of themselves.

Description

Thirty-six opposite or nearly opposite adjectives are given. For each, the student is to mark one of four positions, indicating whether he or she is: "very much like the first adjective," " more like the first than the second," "more like the second than the first," or "very much like the second." An example is: "bold ____ ____ ____ ____ timid." There is just one score, but there are several forms that measure different characteristics. (See "Alternate Forms" below.)

Administration

The instrument can be administered individually or to a group. The instructions are simple and clear. There is no time limit. Most students will finish a single form within five minutes.

Alternate Forms

There are separate sets of forms for adults, students, teachers, and nurses. Each set has several forms. Most of the forms have identical items and differ only in the instructions. For the adult set, there are forms for reporting one's self concept, one's ideal self, one's perceptions of how others perceive one, and others' perceptions of a given person. Most of the forms are available in Spanish, Italian, and French, as well as English.

Reliability

Test-retest reliability after seven or eight weeks has been high (.88). Internal consistency has been high (.79 to .94).

Validity

The student form has correlated moderately (.68) with the Coopersmith Self-Esteem Inventory. The adult form has correlated moderately (.72) with the self-concept score on the Minnesota Multiphasic Personality Inventory.

Scoring & Interpretation

Manual scoring is fairly simple and quick. Marks in the left most position are given +2 points, those in the next positions are given +1, -1, -2, respectively. Then those points are totaled. There is norm data based on several studies with a total of 2,650 persons. Data are reported for small samples of high school students, college students, young urban working adults, factory workers, and business managers. In each case the data are reported separately for men and women, but not by race and ethnicity.

Comments

This instrument was developed for adults. Though the student is only required to read 72 adjectives, the adjectives tend to be long and make fine distinctions. As a consequence, the required reading is at about the eighth grade level. The manual suggests that the instrument can be administered to low readers by having the administrator read the item number and adjectives aloud to the students, but several of the adjectives are likely to be beyond the oral vocabulary of some of the students.

This reviewer finds the scoring of several items to be questionable. For two items, both adjectives seem indicative of a equally positive self image, but one receives positive points and the other receives negative points. In five other items it seems that the healthiest and best functioning people would be about half way between the two adjectives, but people who perceive themselves as such will receive a lower score for self-concept than those who place their marks closest to the positively scored adjective.

It appears that the type of personality that will score high on this instrument is the macho Pollyanna. Community activists, for example, are likely to be judged as having a mediocre self-concept because they tend to be dissatisfied with the existing order, unwilling to accept it, impassioned, and impatient for change. In programs that successfully mobilize the participants to be self-directed in their own lives and that of their community, this instrument probably will show no increase in self-concept and perhaps even a decrease.

Availability

The instrument will be sold to anyone.

Price

The instrument costs $.30 per copy. The manual costs $5.00. A specimen set, including the manual and one copy of each of the eleven adult forms, costs $8.30.

Source

SOARES Associates
111 Teeter Rock Road
Trumbull, CT 06611
(203) 375-5353

Tennessee Self-Concept Scale
(TSCS)

Author & Date
William H. Fitts (1956-84)

Purpose
To assess self-concept.

Description
There are 100 self-descriptive statements. The student responds to each on a five-point scale. The statements are like: "I like myself," "I cannot be trusted," and "I meet my family responsibilities." There are scores for physical self, moral-ethical self, personal self, family self, social self, self criticism, and for total self esteem. There also are scores for perceptions of "What I am," "Satisfaction with myself," and "What I do." Additional scores can be calculated, but they are primarily used for psychotherapeutic diagnosis.

Administration
The instrument can be administered individually or to a group. The instructions are fairly simple and clear. The student book and answer sheet however, are arranged in a manner that is unusual and could cause some students difficulty. The student is to start answering in the right hand column, instead of the left hand one; the first page of the student booklet has consecutive items numbered 1, 3, 5, 19, 21, 23, 37 and so forth; and the right hand column of the answer sheet has the responses for these items on every other line (the consecutive response choices are for items 1, 2, 3, 4, 5, 19, 20, 21, 22, 23, 24, 27 and so forth). The only instruction to the student about answering is, "As you start, be sure that your answer sheet and this booklet are lined up evenly so that the item numbers match each other." Each of the six pages of the booklet have to be aligned both horizontally and vertically on the answer sheet.

There is no time limit. Most students finish within 20 minutes.

Alternate Forms
The are two forms, the Counseling Form and the Clinical and Research Form. Both use the same student booklet, but the latter is scored in a more elaborate manner.

Reliability

Test-retest reliability, after two weeks, has been generally high (mostly .75 to .90).

Validity

The manual does not report correlations between scores on this instrument and scores on other measures of self-concept. Studies have shown that psychiatric patients have lower scores on this instrument than the general population, and that the general population has lower scores than people nominated as unusually healthy personalities. Juvenile delinquents, unwed mothers, and alcoholics all have lower scores than the general population. Most of the scores of the Counseling Form correlate moderately or highly with each other. This suggests that they are not measuring different characteristics and that the total score is the most meaningful one.

Scoring & Interpretation

Manual scoring for the Counseling Form is moderately complex, but each step is clearly shown on a work-sheet to which the student's marks are transferred by carbon paper. The scoring takes about five minutes per person. Manual scoring for the Clinical and Research Form is more complicated and time consuming. Computerized scoring is available from the publisher. Norm data are based on 626 people--black and white, of various ages and socio-economic status. Most studies have shown only small score differences between people with different demographic characteristics.

Comments

This instrument was developed for adolescents and adults. The required reading is at about the sixth grade level. The instrument has been used in hundreds of published studies. A 1985 review (in The Ninth Mental Measurement Yearbook, # 1236) described this as probably the most comprehensively developed measure of self-concept in use today.

Availability

The instrument is sold only to "qualified professional users."

Price

Ten reusable student booklets cost $12.75. Twenty-five answer and profile sheets cost $8.75. The manual, which does not include a copy of the instrument or the answer sheet, but does include an updated bibliography, costs $12.50. The publisher does not sell a specimen set.

Source

Western Psychological Services
12031 Wilshire Blvd.
Los Angeles, CA 90025
(800) 222-2670 or (800) 423-7863 in California

Wahler Self-Description Inventory (WSDI)

Author & Date

H. J. Wahler (1955-1971)

Purpose

To assess the degree to which individuals emphasize favorable and unfavorable characteristics in their self-evaluations.

Description

There are 66 self-description statements. The student responds to each on a nine point scale with 0 representing "Not at all like me," 4 representing "Moderately like me," and 9 representing "Beyond question very much like me." The statements are like: "I am generally happy;" "I feel like I'm getting nowhere in life;" and "I care about other people." There are two scores. One is the average rating given to the positive statements, and the other is the average rating given to the negative statements.

Administration

The instrument can be administered individually or to a group. The instructions are simple and clear. There is no time limit. Most students finish within 15 minutes.

Alternate Forms

There is just one form.

Reliability

Test-retest reliability has been low to high (.43 to .95). The interval of retesting was 1, 2, and 13 weeks, and in each case the values were lower for women than men. KR-20 has been high (.85 to .99).

Validity

The manual provides limited validity data. Studies have shown substantial differences between the scores of college students and adults who seek psychiatric services. When college students who had already completed the instrument were asked to answer it again in terms of how they felt during "one of the most distressful periods of their lives," the average scores on the positive statements declined substantially and the average scores on the negative statements rose substantially. When psychiatric patients were asked to answer again thinking of "one of the best periods of their lives when they were feeling most secure and free of trouble," the average scores changed in the opposite direction.

Scoring & Interpretation

Manual scoring is moderately simple and quick. The ratings of the positive statements are totalled and then divided by the number of such statements answered. The same is done for the negative items. Limited norm data are provided. They are based on 220 junior and senior high school students, 301 college students and 528 adult psychiatric patients. Little information is given about the characteristics of these persons. The manual warns that extremely high scores on favorable statements and low scores on unfavorable statements are probably signs of grandiosity and denial, rather than of a positive self image.

Comments

This instrument was designed for adolescents and adults. The content and tone are adult. The required reading is at about the 6th grade level. A 1978 review (in The Eighth Mental Measurements Yearbook, #2584) concluded that this instrument was amateurishly developed and should not be used.

Availability

This instrument is sold only to "qualified professional users."

Price

One hundred copies of the instrument and answer sheet cost $12.10. The manual costs $6.90. A specimen set is not available, but the manual includes a copy of the instrument.

Source

Western Psychological Services
12031 Wilshire Blvd.
Los Angeles, CA 90025
(800) 222-2670, or (800) 423-7863 in California

Critical
Thinking

Introduction

Critical thinking, as the term is commonly used by adult educators, has two somewhat different meanings. The first is the application of good logic, scientific methods, and argumentation. This involves: careful observation; distinguishing among assumptions, facts, and values; making valid deductions; drawing inferences from given facts; judging the credibility of statements made by others; and recognizing dirty tricks such as irrelevances, circularity in reasoning, and shifts in definition. The second meaning is the application of those skills in the context of value preferences, for the purposes of making decisions about one's life and about social issues.

There are few available instruments for measuring critical thinking. All those located that appeared potentially useful for adult literacy programs focus on the first definition. They require reading at Grades 5 - 9, and cannot be adapted to oral administration for very limited readers. This is because many items require processing considerable information. Even persons who score well usually need to refer back to previously read information before answering many of the items.

Instruments that Measure Critical Thinking

Cornell Critical Thinking Tests (CCTT)

Author & Date
Robert H Ennis & others (1961-85)

Purpose
To measure a broad array of critical thinking skills.

Description
This instrument covers induction, deduction, evaluation of the credibility of observations, and detection of assumptions that underlie conclusions. Level X of the instrument has the student read a science fiction mystery and answer questions about it that require: 1) indicating whether given information "supports" or "goes against" a hypothesis; 2) choosing which of two statements of observation is more "believable;" 3) selecting a valid conclusion for a given major and minor premise of a syllogism; and 4) selecting an assumption underlying a given conclusion. There are 71 items in Level X. Level Y of the instrument has students: 1) read a debate about immigration policy and decide whether the conclusions of the disputants are valid deductions from their premises; 2) read a debate about a health issue and decide why the thinking presented is "faulty;" 3) read about a laboratory experiment and choose which of two statements of observation is more "believable;" 4) indicate whether additionally presented information about the experiment "supports" or "goes against" the original conclusion from it; 5) indicate which predictions are most consistent with a given "if-then" statement based on the experiment; 6) read statements about stock cars and baking, and select the assumption made in word definition when reaching a given conclusion; and 7) read about child raising and select an assumption made in reaching a given conclusion. There are a total of 52 items in Level Y. There is just a single score, the number of items correctly answered.

Administration
The instrument can be administered individually or to a group. The instructions are simple, but the exercises require making some fine distinctions that are not clearly specified in the instructions. There is a time limit of 50 minutes. The manual says 90-95 percent of the students should finish in that time, but this Ph.D. reviewer just barely finished within the limit.

Alternate Forms

There are two levels of the instrument. Level X is suitable for students in grades 5 to 14. Level Y is suitable for gifted high school students, college students, and other adults.

Reliability

Test-retest reliability is not reported in the manual. Split-half reliability has been high for Level X (.76 to .87) and moderate for Level Y (.55 to .76). KR-18, 20, & 21 have been moderate to high (.67 to .90) for Level X and moderate (.50 to .77) for Level Y.

Validity

The correlations of this instrument with other instruments of critical thinking have been low to moderate (mostly between .40 and .50). The other instruments have included the Watson-Glaser Critical Thinking Appraisal, the Logical Reasoning Test, a Test of Critical Thinking, and the Reflective Judgment Interview. The manual does not report correlations between Level X and Level Y.

Scoring & Interpretation

Scoring is simple and quick. The mean scores, standard deviations, and some percentile distributions are reported for 15 classes of high school and college students that took Level X of the instrument and 20 classes of college students that took Level Y. The classes were from several parts of the country.

Comments

The manual carefully articulates what the instrument focuses on measuring and what it does not cover. It states that open-mindedness, caution, and being well-informed are important to critical thinking, but not covered in the instrument. This reviewer thinks that the first two characteristics are measured indirectly; a substantial lack of either is likely to adversely affect a student's score.

The exercises in these instruments are difficult. The average college student only gets about 65 percent of the items correct. A reading level of about the 6th grade is needed for Level X, and a reading level of about the 8th grade is needed for Level Y.

Availability

This instrument will be sold to anyone.

Price

Ten reusable student booklets of either level cost $16.95. Ten machine-scored answer sheets cost $4.95, but are not necessary. The manual costs $6.95. A specimen set, including a copy of the manual, costs $10.00.

Source

Midwest Publications Company
P.O. Box 448
Pacific Grove, CA 93950
(408) 375-2455

Ennis-Weir Critical Thinking Essay Test

Author & Date
Robert H. Ennis & Eric Weir (1983-85)

Purpose
To test critical thinking in the context of written argumentation.

Description
The student is presented with a letter to the editor of a local paper proposing a change in the local parking regulations. The student is to consider the letter "paragraph by paragraph and as a total argument." Then the student is to write a letter to the same editor in response to the given one. For each paragraph read, he or she is to write a paragraph "telling whether you believe the thinking good or bad." The student is also to write a closing paragraph about the entire argument. The student is directed to "Defend your judgments with reasons." Each of the first seven paragraphs of the given letter exhibit different kinds of reasoning errors, but there is just one overall score.

Administration
The instrument can be administered individually or to a group. The instructions are simple and clear. There is a 40 minute time limit for reading the given letter and writing the response.

Alternate Forms
There is only one form.

Reliability
Test-retest and internal reliability are not reported in the manual. When pairs of trained graders scored the same set of tests, their scores correlated highly (.82 and .86). This only indicates that the scoring can be done reliably.

Validity
This instrument has not been validated against other measures of critical thinking. The manual indicates that because of the specificity of the material to which the student is to respond and the variety of acceptable responses, it is difficult to define exactly what the instrument is measuring. But it goes on to suggest that the realism of the task and the inclusion of several important errors of reasoning in the given letter create an opportunity "in which skill at critical thinking ought to manifest itself."

Scoring & Interpretation

Scoring is complex, but the manual states that a trained person needs only five or six minutes for each student's responses. The manual extensively discusses good and poor responses to each paragraph of the given letter. The scoring sheet briefly summarizes what should be in a good response. The manual, however, urges that the grader use flexibility and judgment because "adequate responses may be expressed in different ways...and...critical thinking is an open-ended activity." The grader is also cautioned that credit should not be withheld for poor writing. The manual does not report norms, but it does report the mean and standard deviation for one college class that was half way through an introductory logic course and one class of gifted eighth grade students. (There was a marked difference in the average scores of the two groups.)

Comments

The instrument is adult in content and tone. Some persons who do not own cars or commute to work by automobile may find the content unfamiliar or of little interest. Reading skill of about the seventh grade level is needed.

This instrument assesses critical thinking in one type of real life task, that of criticizing the arguments of others. But it does not assess critical thinking in the more common real life task, that of generating arguments, such as when proposing a new policy or appealing an adverse action. It is not clear that people who are skilled at the former are always skilled at the latter.

Availability

The instrument will be sold to anyone.

Price

The manual, which includes a copy of the instrument and scoring sheet, costs $9.95. The publisher permits purchasers of the manual to reproduce the instrument and scoring sheet for classroom use.

Source

Midwest Publications Company
P.O. Box 448
Pacific Grove, CA 93950
(408) 375-2455

Ross Test of Higher Cognitive Processes

Author & Date
John D. Ross and Catherine M. Ross (1976-86)

Purpose
To assess higher order thinking skills--specifically analysis, synthesis, and evaluation.

Description
The instrument is divided into eight sections, each with eight to eighteen items and a separate score. The first section measures ability to identify analogous relations between sets of words. The second section measures deductive reasoning with items like: "All quarks are meat eaters. Some quarks live in Greenland. Therefore: a) ... b) ... c) ...." The third section measures the ability to identify the missing premise needed to complete a logical syllogism with items like: "The factory is pumping copper waste into the river. (Missing fact). Therefore the factory is killing off the trout. The missing fact is: a) ... b) ... c) ...." The fourth section measures ability to organize and synthesize data. An example is: "Select a word from the given list of twelve that goes with all the following four words in some way: clothes, up, straight, and drive." The answer is "line" because of "clothes line," "line up," "straight line," and "line drive." The fifth section measures the ability to construct a cogent argument by ordering ten given sentences. The sixth section measures inferences from questioning. Six items are given and one of them is IT. There are three sets of three questions with their answers. The student has to infer which item is IT and which of the sets is sufficient, by itself, to determine which item is IT. The seventh section states a mathematics word problem, but the statement may not provide all the information necessary to answer the problem or it may present extraneous information; the student has to decide which is the case. The eighth section measures ability to infer the common and distinguishing attributes of a set of presented figures.

Administration
The instrument can be administered individually or to a group. The instructions are simple and clear. There are time limits that total 2 hours. The time limits are tough for fourth, fifth, and sixth graders; only about 60 percent complete each section.

Alternate Forms
There is only one form.

Reliability

Test-retest reliability has been high (.94). Split-half reliability also has been high (.92).

Validity

Considerable data allegedly supporting the validity of this instrument is reported in the manual, but most of it is weak evidence, at best. The section scores increase with age, IQ, and years of schooling.

Scoring & Interpretation

Manual scoring is simple, but requires four or five minutes per student because of the large number of items. Limited norm data are available. They are based on 1137 students in the fourth, fifth, and sixth grades of nine school districts in the state of Washington. About half the students were identified as gifted; no other information about them is provided in the manual. Norms are reported for each of the eight section scores, as well as for the total score.

Comments

This instrument was developed for youth in grades 4-6. Some of the items are juvenile in content or tone. Sections 1, 4, 6, and 8 have an academic tone, requiring skills that are not commonly used in daily life. The required reading is at about the fifth grade level. This is a tough test for elementary school students. The average forth grader answered only 49 out of 105 items correctly. The average sixth grader answered only 64 of 105 correctly.

The manual alleges that this is a test of cognitive processing, not intelligence, and it reports low correlations with the Lorge-Thorndike Intelligence Test, when calculated separately for non-gifted students and for gift-students, as defined by prior IQ test results. This was an incorrect test of the allegation. The correct calculation would have been for all students together, and that would probably have increased the correlations. In addition, the items in Sections 1 and 8 are identical with those commonly found in intelligence tests.

A 1985 review (in The Ninth Mental Measurements Yearbook, # 1061) found the validity and norm data inadequate.

Availability

This instrument is "restricted to qualified professionals--orders must be placed on official institutional purchase forms or professional letterhead."

Price

Ten reusable student booklets cost $15.00. Twenty-five answer sheets cost $8.00. The manual costs $10.00. A specimen set, including a copy of the manual costs $10.00.

Source

Academic Therapy Publications
20 Commercial Blvd.
Novato, CA 94949-6191
(415) 883-3314

Watson-Glaser Critical Thinking Appraisal (CTA)

Author & Date

Goodwin Watson & Edward Glaser (1942-1980)

Purpose

To measure some of the important skills involved in critical thinking.

Description

There are five sections, each with 16 true-false or multiple-choice items. Section 1 provides three short paragraphs of facts, each followed by several statements of inference. The student is to rate each inference as "definitely true," "probably true," "insufficient data," "probably false," and "definitely false." Section 2 provides five statements, each followed by several assumptions. The student is to indicate whether each assumption was or was not taken for granted in the preceding statement. Section 3 provides six sets of major and minor premises, each followed by several conclusions. The student is to indicate which of the conclusions are necessarily true. Section 4 provides five short paragraphs, each followed by several conclusions. The student is to indicate which conclusion follows from the preceding paragraph; this is a measure of interpretation--weighing evidence and making generalizations. Section 5 provides five controversial questions, each followed by several answers and supporting arguments. The student is to judge whether each argument is a strong or weak one for the preceding question. Just one score is computed, the total number correct.

Administration

The instrument can be administered individually or to a group. The instructions are simple and clear. There is no time limit, but almost all students finish within 40 minutes.

Alternate Forms

There are two equivalent forms, A and B.

Reliability

Test-retest reliability has been moderately high (.73). Split-half reliability has been moderately high (.69 to .85).

Validity

The manual does not report correlations with other measures of critical thinking. The scores do increase moderately for grade levels of high school and years of college, as would be expected. The scores also have improved after courses in critical thinking.

Scoring & Interpretation

Manual scoring is simple and quick. National norm data are reported for each grade of high school. The data are based on almost 7,000 students from 24 school districts in 17 states; eleven percent were members of racial and ethnic minority groups. Performance data are also reported for samples of junior college students, four-year college students, police officers, and sales representatives from a large business machine company.

Comments

This instrument was developed for high school and college students. The content and tone is adult, but rather middle class in orientation. The required reading at about the ninth grade level.

The instrument has been used in hundreds of published studies. In a 1983, a panel of psychologists judged it to be generally superior to the Cornell Critical Thinking Test. A 1984 review (in Test Critiques--Vol. III, pg. 682) said it is the best available instrument for its purpose. A 1985 review (in The Ninth Mental Measurements Yearbook, #1347) confirmed that judgment despite noting some problems. But a second review in the same 1985 source questioned the validity of the instrument and concluded it would be possible to construct a better one.

This instrument explains to the students the types of critical thinking that are to be assessed. For instance, Section 1 begins with a definition of "inference," gives an example of a specific one, and discusses why that inference is reasonable but not certain. It then gives instructions on how to do the exercises, provides an example exercise with the correct answer, and explains the answer. Finally the actual test items are presented. This has the advantage of giving the student a good idea of what will be considered a correct answer. But it also makes some of the students know more about good critical thinking after reading the instructions than they knew immediately before. That could be a problem when using the instrument in a longitudinal study to evaluate the effects of an educational program on students' critical thinking.

Availability

This test will be sold to organizations that have a staff member who has completed an advanced level course in measurement at an accredited college or university.

Price

Thirty-five reusable student booklets cost $54.00. Thirty-five answer sheets cost $17.00. The manual costs $10.00. A specimen set, including a copy of the manual, costs $15.00.

Source

The Psychological Corporation
555 Academic Court
San Antonio, TX 78204-0952
(512) 299-1061

APPENDIX

An extensive search was made between July 1987 and April 1988 for instruments that might be useful for evaluating important outcomes of adult literacy programs. The outcomes of interest were:

reading
writing
mathematics
oral language proficiency of ESL students
assistance in the academic development of one's   children
self-image
self-determination
critical thinking and problem solving
employment status
altruism
community participation and leadership
life-long learning

The search focused on commercial instruments published in the U.S. and on those used by community based literacy programs in the U.S.. Commercial instruments are more likely than non-commercial ones to have been rigorously developed and validated, to be accompanied by norm data, to be available readily in quantity, and to be accompanied by thorough instructions on their use, scoring, and interpretation. Instruments used by community based literacy programs were expected to be creative and promising tools of little renown.

The search for commercial instruments was begun by examining the following guides:

Adult Assessment (Richard S. Andrulis, 1977)

English Language Proficiency Tests (J. Charles Alderson, Karl J. Krahnke, & Charles W. Stansfield (Eds.))

Evaluating Student Performance: A Handbook for Adult Literacy Programs (Susan Koen & M. Musumeci, 1987)

Measuring Human Behavior (Dale G. Lake, Matthew B. Miles, & Ralph B. Earle, 1973)

The Ninth Mental Measurements Yearbook (James V. Mitchell, Jr., 1985)

A Resource Guide of Tests for Adult Basic Education Teachers (Robert W. Zellers, undated--1986 or 1987)

Test Critiques--Vols. 1-3 (Daniel J. Keyer & Richard C. Sweetland, 1984)

Testing Instruments and Procedures for Adult English as a Second Language (Dennis Terdy, Jeff Bright, & Teresa Brecht, 1981)

Tests--2nd Edition (Richard C. Sweetland & Daniel J.Keyer, 1986)

Tests in Print (James V. Mitchell, Jr., 1983)

Tests of Functional Adult Literacy (Dean H. Nafziger, R. Thompson, M. Hiscox, & T. Owen, 1975)

The search of these directories yielded about 100 instruments that appeared potentially useful. Samples of almost all these instruments and copies of their manuals were ordered. About half of the orders were received. In some cases the instruments had been discontinued. In other cases the publishers had moved without forwarding addresses or failed to answer two written inquiries, and did not have a listed phone number in the city of their last known address. It is likely that most of these publishers are out of business.

The search for instruments used by community based literacy programs was done by announcements in the Association of Community Based Education's *CBE Report*, by letters to organizations known to be involved in some form of assessment, and by following up all leads that arose from any source. This search yielded about twenty instruments, about half of which were commercially available and half of which were locally developed. The latter were mostly self-report questionnaires, were considered preliminary means of collecting needed data, were not accompanied by instructions for their administration and scoring, and had not been subject to reliability and validity analyses. Consequently, they are not reviewed in this book.

Relevant Tests That Were Not Reviewed

Adult Basic Reading Inventory, Scholastic Testing Service ... Out of print.

Adult Performance Level, American College Testing Program ... Out of print.

Assessment of Skills in Computation, Los Angeles Unified School District ... Out of print.

Basic Inventory of Academic and Survival Skills ... Out of print.

Basic Inventory of Natural Language, Charles Herbert & others

Basic Occupational Literacy Test, U.S. Employment Service ... This instrument is used by state
    Employment Security Agencies and is not available for use by others. The scores on this
    instrument correlate moderately to highly with corresponding scores on the Test of Adult
    Basic Education, which is reviewed above.

Basic Skills for Critical Thinking, Gary McCuen ... Out of Print

Basic Skills Reading Mastery Test, University of Wisconsin--Extension ... Out of print.

Bernreuter Personality Inventory, Stoelting Company ... Out of print.

Bilingual Oral Language Test, Sam Cohen & others ... Could not locate publisher.

Bilingual Syntax Measure II, Marina Burt & others

California Test of Personality, Louis Thorpe & others ... Obsolete.

Comprehensive English Language Test for Speakers of English as a Second Language, David Harris
    & Leslie Palmer ... Out of print.

Comprehensive Personal Assessment System: Self Report Inventory, Oliver Bown .. This
    instrument was developed to assess teacher trainees' attitudes toward self, their parents,
    young children, authority figures, work, life's uncertainties, their future, etc.

Comprehensive Tests of Basic Skills, CTB/McGraw-Hill ... This is a widely used elementary and
    secondary school achievement test. It takes 5 hours to administer.

Critical Reasoning Test Battery: Verbal Evaluation ... British publisher.

Delta Oral Placement Test, Sandra Berkly & Gary Moore

The Empathy Test, W. A. Kerr & B. J. Speroff ... Could not locate the publisher.

English Language Skills Assessment in a Reading Context, Donna Ilyin ... Out of print.

English Reading Test for Students of English as a Foreign Language, Harold King and Russel
    Campbell ... Could not locate the publisher.

Everyday Skills Test, CTB/McGraw-Hill ... Out of print.

Examination in Structure, Charles Fries & Robert Lado ... Out of print.

General Tests of English Language Proficiency, TENEC International ... Must be administered by agents of the publisher.

Henderson-Moriarty ESL Placement Test, Cindy Henderson & Pia Moriarty ... For Southeast Asian refugees; requires bilingual administrator.

Idea Proficiency Test II, Enrique Dalton & Beverly Amori

Ilyin Oral Interview, Donna Ilyin ... Out of print.

Individual Reading Placement Inventory ... Out of print.

Industrial Reading Test, The Psychological Corporation ... The emphasis is on content about industrial manufacturing processes.

Interagency Language Roundtable Oral Proficiency Interview, U.S. Interagency Language Roundtable ... Also known as the OI or Language Proficiency Interview; is a general system for assessing oral language proficiency in any language; requires 3 - 5 days of training.

Iowa Tests of Basic Skills, A. N. Hieronymus & others ... This is a widely used elementary and secondary school achievement test.

Lado Test of Aural Comprehension, Robert Lado ... Out of print.

Life Themes Inventory, Kelly Bennett & others ... Could not locate the publisher.

Listening Comprehension Picture Test, Donna Ilyin

Logical Reasoning, Alfred Hertzka & J. P. Guilford ... Requires equivalent of ninth grade education.

Maculaitis Assessment Program, Jose Cruz-Matos and others ... The publisher does not sell a specimen set.

Mastery: Survival Skills Tests, Science Research Associates ... Out of print.

Mutually Responsible Facilitation Inventory, T. D. Gnagey ... Could not locate the publisher.

National Assessment of Educational Progress: Young Adult Literacy Assessment, Irwin Kirsch & others ... The instrument used in this widely publicized study has several commendable features, but it is not available for use by others.

Oral Rating Form for Rating Language, Proficiency in Speaking and Understanding English, David Harris ... Distribution is restricted to government agencies.

Peace Corp Language Proficiency Interview, Foreign Service Institute ... Could not locate.

P-Oral Placement Test for Adults, Allen Ferrel ... Publisher did not provide a review copy.

Quick Language Assessment Inventory, Steven Moreno ... Does not measure English language proficiency, but rather predicts it based on place of birth, place of education, and other socio-cultural characteristics.

Rotter Incomplete Sentences Blank, Julian Rotter ... This instrument is used primarily to measure maladjustment and must be interpreted by a psychologist or psychiatrist.

Scales of Independent Behavior, Robert Bruininks & others ... This instrument is primarily used to assess elementary life skills of handicapped children and adults.

Self Assessment Scales, Ardyth Norem-Hebeisen ... Could not locate the publisher.

Steck-Vaughn Placement Survey for Adult Basic Education ... Out of print; a new revision will be released in late 1988.

Structure Tests--English Language, Jeanette Best and Donna Ilyin ... Out of print.

Survival Skills in Reading and Mathematics, Science Research Associates ... Out of print.

Test of Cognitive Skills, CTB/McGraw Hill ... This is designed to assess a student's academic aptitude. There are four kinds of items: identification of patterns in sequences; identification of literal or symbolic relationships in analogies; memorization of definitions of new words; and verbal reasoning -- classifying according to common attributes, inferring relationships among words, identifying essential aspects of objects or concepts, and drawing logical conclusions from short passages.

Test of English Proficiency Level, George Rathmell

Tests of General Educational Development, American Council on Education ... This is what is more commonly known as the GED test. It is available only at authorized GED test centers. The Official GED Practice Test is reviewed in this book.

Ullman ESL Achievement Test for Beginning ESL Students, Ann Ullman ... Out of print.

Wisconsin Test of Adult Basic Education, University of Wisconsin--Extension ... Out of print.

WRITE: Junior and Senior High, Los Angeles Unified School District ... Out of print.

Writing Proficiency Program, Richard Bossone ... Out of print.
Index of Tests

Index of Adult Literacy Tests not included

Index of Tests